FEELING GOOD

The Secret To Manifesting

Kenneth Wong

Cover design by: Kenneth Wong
Cover photo by: Marlon Martinez

ISBN: 978-1-7775529-0-9

Feeling good is your birthright.

The moment you reclaim your ability to feel good is the moment you unlock the door to manifesting a life beyond your wildest dreams.

CONTENTS

Title Page 1
Copyright 2
Epigraph 3
Introduction 7
Chapter 1: You Can Feel Good Right Now 9
Chapter 2: Energy Is All Around Us 22
Chapter 3: The Law of Attraction 31
Chapter 4: Manifesting 39
Chapter 5: Raise Your Vibration 51
Chapter 6: Protect Your Vibration 61
Chapter 7: Miracles 69
Chapter 8: Obstacles Are Opportunities 76
Chapter 9: Follow Your Passion 83
Chapter 10: Be the Light 90
Acknowledgments 97
About the Author 99
Notes 101

INTRODUCTION

I am beyond excited for you to read this book on manifestation. Even before I completed the manuscript, I had a feeling that this book will greatly serve the world because I can sense a new generation of spiritual seekers who are awakening all across the globe. Manifesting has been floating around the zeitgeist for a while now, but its popularity is at an all-time high as a result of social media. Millions of people, especially the younger generation, are beginning to realize the powers that they hold within them.

From creating vision boards to writing positive affirmations, new seekers are eager to manifest. But at the same time, many new seekers give up on manifesting because they aren't seeing any results from their actions. I resonate with this feeling on a personal level because I was there once. I was under the limiting belief that like all things in life, I had to work hard in order to manifest. But no matter how many times I meditated, journaled, or recited affirmations, I still couldn't manifest what I wanted. Looking back now, I can pinpoint exactly where the problem was. I was so focused on what I needed to do; I neglected the most important component to manifesting—my feelings.

Manifesting is not about what you do, but how you feel. Our external circumstances are *always* direct reflections of our internal state. When you shift your perception, the world around you shifts accordingly. In other words, you always manifest the emotions you feel. Therefore, feeling good is a *prerequisite* to manifesting what you want. You must feel good *before* you can manifest.

Not the other way around. Understanding this truth completely transformed my manifestation practice. When you commit to make feeling good your highest priority, you will manifest everything you desire and more.

But life is unpredictable and there will be many curveballs along the way (*um hello—global pandemic*), so we cannot just depend on our external circumstances to make us feel good. But the good news for us is, there is a better way. There is an ever-present, all-encompassing force of love that we can access at any time. This higher power goes by many names including the Universe, God, and Source. No matter what name you use, simply know that we are all referring to this same force of love.

Tuning into this force of love helps us see beyond the physical plane and gives us access to spiritual solutions. By leaning on a higher power, you have a reliable way to feel good no matter what life throws at you. When you cultivate a spiritual connection with a God of your own understanding, you gain the ability to co-create a life that you love. This co-creation process is more commonly known as manifestation. But manifesting is more than just a genie lamp to get what you want. Manifesting is a spiritual way of life that involves aligning your thoughts, feelings, and emotions with the loving force of the Universe, who then works with you to co-create a life beyond your wildest dreams.

Through reading this book, you will come to learn that manifesting is not just about getting what you want. But rather a moment-by-moment practice of choosing better-feeling thoughts, so that you can manifest what is of the highest good for all. Feeling good is the secret to manifesting, hence the title of this book. But this book is more than just a guide on teaching you how to feel good. It's about reclaiming it—for the ability to feel good never left you. You just need to remember it. It's time to get out of your own way and rediscover the hidden power within you.

CHAPTER 1: YOU CAN FEEL GOOD RIGHT NOW

I was 21, fresh out of college, and I just landed a full-time position in accounting. To people on the outside, I was your typical young professional who was learning the ropes and trying to get his career started. But on the inside, I was a complete mess. I was anxious, depressed, and I frequently experienced panic attacks that paralyzed me mentally and physically. I knew I should be grateful for even having a job in the first place but the daily routine of working nine to five took a toll on my mental health. I couldn't help but think to myself, "Is this all there is to life?" Every day I would come home with more complaints and more reasons to feel bad about my life. Feeling good seemed like a distant memory.

It was at this point in my life that I became interested in the Law of Attraction and the concept of manifesting. The promise that I could get whatever I thought about was the perfect solution to my problems, or so I thought. I looked frantically at my external circumstances to see what I needed to fix in my life. My first target was my job. I didn't get along well with my boss, so I blamed my job for making me feel depressed. I was determined to manifest a new job. At this point in my manifestation journey, I was under the impression that the more I thought about my new job, the faster I could manifest it. I spent every waking moment obsessing over my career and I scripted affirmations like "I want a new job" every day after work. But nothing worked. Every interview I went to always ended up with me being turned down for the position. Every rejection left me feeling worse and worse and I felt out of control of the trajectory of my career.

When I failed to control my external circumstances, I turned to the only thing that I could control which was my weight. I put myself on a low-calorie diet and I created self-imposed restrictions on what I could or could not eat. I was not overweight by any standard. In fact, most people would consider me as a skinny guy leaning toward the underweight side. But losing weight wasn't the point. I didn't restrict my diet because I wanted to lose weight. What I wanted the most was to feel good. And being able to control my weight and make the numbers slowly come down made me feel that way. I was willing to starve my own body in exchange for a semblance of control that made me feel better about myself.

It got to a point where I was so depressed and physically ill that I knew I had to stop before I seriously injure myself. I decided that I have had enough and that there must be a better way. At that moment, I felt guided to do something that I haven't done in a long time and that was to pray. I said, "Universe, God, or whoever is out there, I am ready to be free from these negative thoughts. I want to feel good right now." A miraculous shift happened the moment I said that prayer. Having been exposed to organized religion as a young child, I have said prayers in the past, but this time it was different. The energy from the words resonated with the core of my being and I felt an overwhelming sense of peace rush all over me. It was as if I have reignited a dormant connection to my superpower.

This prayer was more than just a cry for help. It created a seismic shift in my perception. I realized that all along I was holding the key to feeling good. The feeling that I desperately longed for was right here at my fingertips. I didn't have to change or fix anything in my life in order to feel good. I simply needed to choose it. The moment I redirected my search for feeling good from the outside to the inside, I felt at peace. I now understand that this shift in perception is the power of aligning with a higher power that transcends the physical realm.

Although my external experiences didn't change immediately, the way I experienced my experiences changed radically. I no longer felt like the victim of my own life. I gave up the need to search for feeling good because I knew that I could choose to tap into this feeling any time I please. Once I realized the immense power my thoughts held, I vowed to never let myself down again. When I became unapologetic about my ability to feel good, my external environment began to transform along with it. My determination to feel good elevated every single area of my life. Everything that I previously pushed so hard for fell into my lap effortlessly. I negotiated a transfer to another department at work. I earned a promotion and a raise. I formed genuine connections with my new colleagues. And most importantly, I was able to find inner peace for the first time in a long time.

Do you want to experience this radical shift in your life? Well, you most certainly can because this superpower is within all of us. At any point in time, we can choose to tune into this higher power who has the ability to change our circumstances, experiences, and outcomes. When you align with a power greater than yourself, you can find relief from negative thoughts and feel better instantly. You can transcend the smallness of the logical mind and reunite with the loving presence of a God of your own understanding. The logical mind is limited because it can only look externally for things that make you feel good. But if you wait for your external circumstances to give you a reason to feel good, you might be stuck waiting for a long time. But the good thing is you don't have to wait until everything is picture perfect before you can feel good. The key to feeling good is to want it. No matter where you are currently in life, your connection to an ever-present stream of well-being is there waiting for you on standby. Feeling good is not a privilege, it is your birthright. The moment you reclaim your ability to feel good is the moment you unlock the door to manifesting a life beyond your wildest dreams.

THE KEY TO MANIFESTING IS TO FEEL GOOD

The number one key to manifesting is to feel good. You manifest what you feel, not what you do. The way you feel is an absolute indicator of the outcomes of your manifestations. I learned this lesson the hard way by trying to force my manifestation to happen. This was the reason why I couldn't manifest a new job despite obsessing over it and writing affirmations every day. I thought I was doing all the right things, but I neglected a key component to manifesting which was my feelings.

Throughout the entire manifestation process, I felt desperate and depressed. The more I pushed for what I wanted, the more frustrated I felt. As a result, I just ended up manifesting more negative outcomes that matched how I felt.

But when I committed to feeling good and realigned with my higher power, I manifested everything I wanted and more. I did not have to push, control, or do anything special. My good feelings alone were enough to manifest my desires.

So, if you want to manifest what you want, you must make it your top priority to feel good. And the only way to consistently feel good is to unsubscribe from the false beliefs of the ego and realign with the loving presence of your inner guide.

THE EGO AND THE INNER GUIDE

Your mind has two ways of thinking. A mindset of love, which is known as the *inner guide*. And a mindset of fear, which is known as the *ego*. I ask that you stay with me even if the language sounds a bit foreign to you. These are key concepts that will recur throughout the book because they are vital for the manifesting process. I promise it's worth it.

The *inner guide* is the love-based mindset that was placed into us by a higher power. The inner guide is always communicating with you through your feelings. Your inner guide only wants the best for you, so it is always pointing you toward what feels good. This is why every single individual on this planet has a natural desire to feel good. Since this mindset of love was created by a higher power, it can see beyond the physical realm and direct you to seek spiritual solutions. Your inner guide knows that the key to feeling good lies within you. When you commit to feeling good by surrendering to a force greater than you, you reconnect with the presence of a higher power—the powerful force that makes all manifestations happen. When you are in alignment with this higher power, you gain the ability to co-create and manifest the experiences you want.

The *ego* is the fear-based mindset that seeped into us as a result of the world we live in. Since the ego was created by the fears of the world, it only knows how to seek physical solutions. The ego convinces you into believing that the key to feeling good exists outside of you, so you spend your whole life chasing after this feeling while remaining under its control. Even if this mentality means going down paths of self-destruction, the ego will continue to push its agenda in order to survive. The ego's only purpose is self-preservation. The ego cannot coexist with the presence of your inner guide, so it pollutes your mind with negative thoughts in order to weaken your connection to your inner guide.

The ego and the inner guide are in a constant battle over your mind. You were born with an innate connection to your inner guide, but the grasp of the ego grows stronger as you grow up because our world prioritizes fear over love. We unconsciously pick up on the fears that run rampant in our homes, societies, media, cultures, and religions. Over time, we forget our connection to our inner guide, and we come to rely on the ego for a false sense of protection. However, the connection to our inner guide may only be forgotten but never destroyed. It is always working behind the scenes to remind us of our truth—which is to feel good. And the moment you recognize that the key to feeling good lies within you, you reconnect with the God of your own understanding. In the presence of your inner guide, the ego is forced to take a backseat because the two cannot coexist.

FEELING GOOD IS FEELING GOD

Fear has become an epidemic in our generation. Even though you may not realize it, the ego has us all living under the grasp of fear every day. Some of you may deny this and think, "What? I don't live in fear! I go to work, I go to the gym, I take care of my family, I..."

Now I don't disagree with the fact that you are a high-functioning human being, but the fear I'm referring to here is *not* the fight-or-flight kind of fear. Fear manifests itself in many forms such as worry, anxiety, depression, unworthiness, and jealousy. All of these negative feelings are rooted in fear.

Many of us have grown accustomed to fear and accepted it as part of who we are. Our society as a collective has accepted feeling bad as the new normal. Just take one look at the news, and you'll witness an overwhelming amount of negativity that is permeating our airwaves every second.

Instead of looking inward to find joy and happiness, the ego tells us to look externally to find moments of relief. Whether it be drugs, sex, alcohol, or in my case—extreme diets, we find our own ways to chase this high. We crave these moments of feeling good so badly that we are willing to trade our physical and mental health in exchange for these fleeting moments of relief.

We have forgotten how natural it is to feel good. But I want to remind you that feeling good is your birthright. You were born to feel joyful, happy, and peaceful. All it takes is a willingness to choose it by surrendering your fear to the Universe and claiming joy as your purpose. When you feel good, you realign with the God that exists *within* you. When you feel good, you feel God.

A GOD OF YOUR OWN UNDERSTANDING

There are no rules when it comes to connecting with a higher power. What matters is you can cultivate a spiritual relationship with a God of your own understanding. You are free to refer to this higher power as the Universe, God, Source, Spirit, Inspiration, or any other name that resonates with you. I prefer to use the name, Universe, but you are free to choose your own. The most important thing here is you are comfortable with the name. No matter what you choose to call this higher power, know that we are all referring to the same, ever-present, all-encompassing force of love that is all around us and within us.

The reason why I want to address this topic is because I know that the name, *God*, is a trigger for a lot of people. Whether this is due to traumatic past experiences or an unpleasant religious upbringing, I want to reassure you that whatever reason you have is absolutely true and valid. Honor your preferences and simply let your intuition guide you to a name that resonates with you.

Many people get hung up on using the proper name, but this is just one of the ego's sneaky ways to distract you from building a spiritual relationship of your own understanding. It doesn't matter what name you use as long as it feels good. After all, feeling good is the foundation of spiritual alignment.

THE GOD WITHIN YOU

Many people have this common misconception that God is an entity that exists *outside* of us. That there is this man sitting in heaven who is judging your every move and action. That you will be sent to heaven or hell depending on what you do in this lifetime. But this is just a false narrative that is perpetuated (usually by people in positions of authority or power) to keep the rest of the population small and under control.

Does it feel good to live a life that's full of restrictions? Does it feel good to live in fear of eternal death? Does it feel good to be judged on everything you say or do? If you answered no to any of these questions, then I have good news for you. This belief in a judgmental God is nothing more than a thought. And like all thoughts, you can always choose to think another one.

The truth is you are an *extension* of God. It's not a mere coincidence that so many people have sought after a higher power for centuries. The need to find God transcends all geographical boundaries, languages, generations, cultures, and religions because the inner guide is within all of us. The inner guide is the spark of God within us. It's the desire within you to feel good. The inner knowing that there's more to life than this. The compass that guides you toward the spiritual realm.

When you say *yes* to your inner guide and reclaim your connection to the Universe, you become powerful beyond measure. When you remember that God doesn't exist *outside* of you but *within* you, you activate your superpower. You open the floodgates to an ever-present stream of love. In the presence of love, you are able to perceive obstacles as opportunities. You are able to perceive difficulties as lessons. You are able to perceive the people in your life as assignments. And most of all, you can feel good knowing you are one with the Universe. Alignment with the Universe is the key to manifesting your desires. It's time to wake up. It is time to unsubscribe from all the beliefs that do not serve you and redefine what God means to you.

YOU ARE NOT YOUR THOUGHTS

One of the biggest lies the ego tries to tell us is to convince us that we are our thoughts. Not only do we sabotage ourselves by thinking thoughts like "I am not good enough," but we also believe in them. When you believe that you are your thoughts, you give up the ability to control whether to think thoughts that make you feel good or thoughts that make you feel bad. In doing so, you give up the ability to manifest intentionally.

Your first reaction reading this may be, "But I am my thoughts! How can thoughts enter my mind if I didn't create them?" When I first learned about this concept, I had the same reaction as you. But I can prove it to you. Take a moment and do this exercise with me right now. I want you to close your eyes and simply direct your attention to your breath. Your goal is to let go of all thoughts and just sit in stillness for five minutes. Breathe in and out slowly but keep your focus on your breathing only. When the five minutes are up, you can keep on reading.

What did you notice during the last five minutes? Was it difficult to not think about anything? Did you notice any random thoughts enter or leave your mind? If at any point during this exercise, you noticed that your attention has drifted off to a random thought. Then you just proved my point. You and your thoughts are a classic example of the subject-object relationship. In this exercise, you were the subject, and the thoughts were the objects. Just the fact that you were able to witness your thoughts moving in and out of your mind proves that you are not your thoughts. For it is impossible for a subject to witness an object unless they are two separate and distinct entities.

You are not your thoughts. You are the consciousness that witnesses every thought. Once you realize that you are separate from your thoughts, you can regain control of your thought system by actively replacing the thoughts that hold you down with better-feeling thoughts that lift you up. Thoughts that bring you into alignment with the loving energy of the Universe.

THINK YOUR WAY INTO ALIGNMENT

Another point of this exercise was to demonstrate the fact that you are always thinking thoughts, whether you want to or not. It's almost impossible to prevent thoughts from forming because most thoughts come and go involuntarily. Every thought has a positive or negative impact on how you feel. So basically, every thought you have either brings you closer into alignment with the Universe or pushes you away from the Universe.

Thoughts are usually direct reflections of your external circumstances. This is why we think more positively and feel good when life is going well, and why we think negatively and fall apart when life gets challenging. This ebb-and-flow causes you to jump in and out of alignment with the Universe which weakens your ability to manifest consistently.

But now that you understand that you are the consciousness that sits behind your thoughts. You can begin to think your way into alignment. That's right. It may be difficult to prevent thoughts from forming, but that doesn't stop you from replacing the current thought with a better-feeling one. Thoughts are just thoughts. They are not permanent. They are not set in stone. You can always choose a better feeling thought. So, if you want to stay in alignment with the Universe, all you have to do is to witness your thoughts, pay attention to how they make you feel, and replace negative thoughts by thinking more positive ones.

Navigating your thought system is like walking through a maze. You might accidentally choose a path that leads to a dead end, but you are always free to backtrack and guide yourself to another path that brings you closer to where you want to go. The only thing you need to do is to recognize that the only person stopping you from backtracking and choosing another path is you! Just as I chose to follow the destructive path of starving my body in order to feel good, I was always free to choose another path that better served me. The moment I stopped identifying with my negative thoughts, I was able to step back and choose better-feeling thoughts that put me back into alignment with the love of the Universe.

Regardless of what happens in your external circumstances, you are always in control of what you think and how you feel about it. When you remember that feeling good is a choice that you make, you reclaim the ability to realign with the Universe any time you please. In this aligned state, you can co-create what you want with the Universe and manifest miracles into your reality.

THREE STEPS TO FEELING GOOD

Now let's get to the fun part! There are many ways available to replace negative thoughts with more positive ones, but I always come back to these three steps. These are what I call the Three Steps To Feeling Good. You can use this method to release the thoughts that do not serve you so that you can come back into alignment with the Universe.

When you are first starting, you may find it helpful to write down your thoughts in a journal so you can gain clarity on how you are feeling. But as you get better at replacing your thoughts, this method will become so second nature to you that you can do it in your mind.

STEP 1: CALL IT OUT

The first step to feeling good is to call out your negative thoughts and how they make you feel.

Take a moment and notice if there are any thoughts in your mind that are causing a disturbance in your emotions. Write down these thoughts in your journal.

When you look a negative thought in the eye, you take away its power because you remember that you are not it. You are the observer that sits behind all of these thoughts; otherwise, you would not be able to witness them in the first place.

STEP 2: FLIP IT UPSIDE DOWN

The next step is to flip that negative thought upside down. Next to each negative thought in your journal, write down the positive thought that you want to feel instead.

This step is actually easier than you think because feeling bad is the exact opposite of feeling good. You don't have to fear your negative thoughts. You can use them as your compass back to feeling good.

Instead of getting upset at your negative thoughts, thank them for showing you how you want to feel. Negative thoughts show you what you don't want, so you can clarify what it is that you do want.

STEP 3: SURRENDER IT TO THE UNIVERSE

Once you have clarity over how you want to feel, it's time to surrender your negative thoughts to the Universe through prayer.

In your journal, write down this prayer and say to yourself, "Universe, I'm ready to let go of these negative thoughts. I choose to feel good right now."

Throughout the book, I will use prayers as a way to help you shift your perspective away from physical solutions and toward spiritual solutions. The act of praying may seem intimidating at first. But prayer is just another word for communication. If you feel some resistance toward praying, simply recognize that it is your ego's resistance to this new method of feeling good.

Prayers are so powerful because they can shift your energy in an instant and reconnect you with the Universe. Think of prayer as a positive affirmation on steroids. Prayer takes affirmations to the next level by directly affirming how you want to feel to a higher power. When you pray, you are not just sending the message to yourself. You are sending the message to the Universe.

The key to prayer is to do it often, not just when you need something. Are you more likely to respond to a friend who only reaches out in difficult times or a friend who is always there for you? Treat your relationship with the Universe like a two-way street and you will feel supported in your daily life.

ARE YOU READY TO FEEL GOOD?

Whenever fear has you in a headlock, you can come back to this chapter and practice the Three Steps To Feeling Good. The more you use it, the easier it becomes to replace your negative thoughts with positive ones. With enough practice, it will become your default state to feel good and align with the Universe.

I want to emphasize that choosing to feel good doesn't mean you ignore your negative feelings or bypass your negative thoughts. Instead, it is a moment-by-moment practice of witnessing your negative thoughts and taking action to shift your perspective to a better place.

Charles R. Swindoll once famously said, "Life is 10% what happens to you and 90% how you react to it." No matter what you go through in life, you always have a choice in how you react to it. And *that* is your superpower. By making positive shifts to your internal state, your external environment will begin to shift along with it.

In the following chapter, I will introduce you to the concept of energy and how it is affected by the Law of Attraction—the most powerful law in the universe. The key to manifesting your desires using the Law of Attraction is to emit highly positive energy through your thoughts, feelings, and emotions. This is why it is so important to start off this book by learning how to feel good because it is the fundamental backbone of all the spiritual concepts that are to come.

It's okay if placing your faith in a higher power is a completely new concept to you. Every chapter in this book is designed to help you discover new methods that will deepen your faith in the Universe. Trust that just by simply picking up this book, you're sending a massive statement to the Universe that you are ready to feel good, realign, and claim your manifesting power.

CHAPTER 2: ENERGY IS ALL AROUND US

Before we dive into the Law of Attraction, we need to take a little detour into something we're all so familiar with—energy. Let's take a pause here because I'm sure some of you may be shaking your heads right now saying, "I have no idea what you're talking about? What the hell is energy?" But let me reassure you that you absolutely do know it. In fact, the reason why you think you don't know it is because you know it so well that it is second nature to you.

Let me illustrate the concept of energy using some everyday examples. You know when you meet someone for the first time, and you can immediately sense they have "good vibes", so you instantly hit it off with them? Or when you go on that first date and you feel your date is giving off "bad vibes", and you can't wait to think of an excuse and get the hell out of there? Well, these feelings are not just your brain playing tricks on you. They are the direct results of your energy receptor (also known as your inner guidance system) doing its job.

Understanding energy is crucial to using the Law of Attraction which basically states that like attracts like. We have all heard of success stories of people using the Law of Attraction to manifest their thoughts into physical reality. But the real attraction behind this phenomenon actually happens on an energetic level. When people say, "You attract what you are," they are not referring to your physical body. They are referring to the energy that's being emitted through your thoughts, feelings, and emotions. If you want to practice the Law of Attraction, you must get used to seeing the world in terms of energy so you can align with the energy of your desires and attract it into your reality.

You can think of this chapter as a primer for what's to come. The goal of this chapter is to crack you open to the concept of energy and help you become more aware of the energy that's all around you and within you. Many of us have been unknowingly carrying limiting beliefs that are sapping our energy every day. But once you open your eyes and perceive everything from the lens of energy, you will be able to eliminate those limiting beliefs that are holding your energy down and restore your energetic state. Regaining control over your energy will be one of the greatest tools you will need to manifest using the Law of Attraction.

EVERYTHING IS ENERGY

To use the Law of Attraction, you need to understand that energy is all around us and within us. We are beings of energy living in a world made up of energy. Everything in this world is emitting a specific frequency of energy at all times. This applies to tangible things such as your phone, car, and house and intangible things such as your thoughts, feelings, and emotions.

Although energy is not something physical that we can see, hear, touch, taste, or smell, we can all feel it. It is an intangible force that can only be sensed by the core of our being.

Even though we are physical beings living in a physical reality, energy is one of the few non-physical things that is universally understood by us. It doesn't matter how old you are, where you were born, or what language you speak. The ability to feel energy is innate within us. In other words, you don't need to be taught how to feel energy—you just do.

LOVE IS THE GREATEST ENERGY

Still not convinced that energy is real? Well, let's talk about everyone's favorite topic—love. A universal energy that we all know and are familiar with is love. Love is an energy that transcends races, cultures, languages, generations, and religions. It is a universal feeling that is understood and desired by all human beings.

Love is intangible. You cannot see it. You cannot touch it. You cannot hear it. You cannot taste it. You cannot smell it. Yet we all know how good it feels to give and receive love. Love contains such intense energy that it can manifest itself physically through a wave of warm and fuzzy feeling that runs through the entire body. The energy of love is so powerful because it is one of the most positive energy with the highest vibrational frequencies that exists. (Don't worry if you aren't familiar with the term *vibration*, you'll learn all about it in Chapter 3.)

This is why in many religions and spiritual teachings; love is synonymous with God. If you struggle with understanding the concept of God, you can simply imagine the highest, purest, and most abundant stream of love that is all around you and within you. Draw on your past experiences when you experienced love, (this love can be from friendships, family, or romantic partners), and imagine it multiplied 1,000 times. This tremendous stream of energy is the essence of the Universe. Love is the Universe. The Universe is love.

THERE ARE ONLY TWO KINDS OF ENERGY

There is a plethora of names we can use to describe different kinds of energy, but there are really only two kinds of energy. Ones that feel good, and ones that feel bad. And the reason why your feelings react when you experience energies is all thanks to your inner guidance system. Your inner guidance system is always working behind the scenes to translate the energy around you into feelings. And the way you feel is an absolute indicator of your alignment with the Universe.

Examples of energies that feel good are love, joy, gratitude, appreciation, and passion. These energies feel good because they are in alignment with your inner guide. Your inner guide's only job is to help you feel good and bring you into alignment with the Universe. When you experience these types of energy, the inner guide translates them into good feelings. Good feelings are the inner guide's way of telling you, "More of this energy please." Because when you dwell in these positive energies, you are in alignment with the Universe.

Examples of energies that feel bad are anxiety, jealousy, depression, unworthiness, and hatred. These energies feel bad because they are out of alignment with your inner guide. When you experience these types of energy, the inner guide translates them into bad feelings because they create misalignment with the Universe. Bad feelings are the inner guide's way of telling you, "Less of this energy please." Because when you dwell in these negative energies, you are out of alignment with the Universe.

We'll get deeper into the specific emotions behind these energies in Chapter 3, but for now, the goal is just to become more aware of the energy that's around you by paying attention to your feelings and leaning into your inner guidance system.

FOLLOW YOUR INTUITION

The ego may be good at manipulating your thoughts, but your inner guide absolutely dominates when it comes to your feelings. Your inner guide is your God-given ability to sense energy and discern between energies that feel good and energies that feel bad. It is the instrument that the Universe uses to guide, lead, and beckon you toward realignment with the truth of who you are.

These feelings often come to us in the form of intuition. Our intuition is always guiding us toward what we truly want, which is to feel good. Intuition comes so quickly and directly that it often precedes your analytical thoughts. Take the example I gave earlier, when you meet someone new, your intuition instantly lets you feel someone's vibe. This hit of inner knowing can occur way before your brain is even done processing what the person is saying.

Throughout your lifetime, your body has been through countless changes. From a little baby to a young child to a full-grown adult, your body has experienced continuous growth and transformation. But your intuition and its ability to translate energy into feelings remain intact. You didn't have to learn it because you were born with it. Children naturally gravitate toward things that bring them joy because they are deeply connected to their intuition. But as you grow up, you begin to resist your intuition because the fearful voice of the ego convinces you to rely on your thoughts and external factors to support your decisions instead.

Your intuition is never wrong because energy never lies. But because of free will, whatever you decide to do after your intuition has spoken is still up to you. More often than not, we ignore the voice of our intuition and let our thoughts get in the way. The good news is your inner guide never gives up on you. It is always sensing, interpreting, and translating the energy around you into feelings and sending this guidance to you in the form of intuition. You just need to listen to it.

FEELING GOOD IS YOUR DEFAULT

Although you may have forgotten this truth, your default state of energy is to feel good. Think about newborn babies and how their only job in life is to feel good by eating, playing, and sleeping. When they do not feel good, they will immediately cry out for attention without any form of hesitation. This is a simple but profound example of the way it should be handled when it comes to responding to our energy. But unfortunately, many of us have been taught the exact opposite during our childhood. We were told to ignore our feelings. We were told to ignore our impulses. We were told to ignore our intuition. And thus, we grow into adults who accept feeling bad as the new normal. We tolerate feeling bad until we break down physically and mentally.

The best way to illustrate your default energetic state is to imagine a rubber duck that's floating on the surface of the water in a bathtub. The rubber duck represents your energetic set point, and the level of water is the measure of your energetic state, with feeling good at the surface and feeling bad at the bottom.

The rubber duck naturally floats on top of the water. That is your natural, good, positive energetic state that you were born with. Notice how it does not need to be taught how to float; it simply does.

Over time, the rubber duck is slowly pushed down into the water by a pair of hands. This downward pressure represents the limiting beliefs that you pick up throughout your lifetime. Limiting beliefs are any beliefs that constrain your life in some way, shape, or form. These beliefs do not serve you and they are the by-products of your negative experiences or traumatic events. Limiting beliefs are often picked up during childhood. As you are rapidly exposed to the world around you through your parents, friends, school, and other life experiences, you begin to pick up false beliefs that go against your natural inclination to feel good. These beliefs can be something minor like feeling left out at school to something major like feeling you are unworthy of happiness. If unconfronted, the effects of limiting beliefs snowball over time which eventually cause you to forget your default energetic state of feeling good.

So now it raises the question, how can the rubber duck rise back to the surface? The answer is simpler than you think. You simply lift the pair of hands that's holding it down. And yes—those hands are your hands. Regardless of how those limiting beliefs came about, you need to realize that the only person holding on to them is you. It may be painful to witness and face your limiting beliefs, but by taking responsibility for holding on to them, you will realize that you are the only one who can save yourself.

No matter what stage you are in life, it's never too late to shed your limiting beliefs. You can begin right here right now as long as you are willing. It's time for you to free yourself from your limiting beliefs and reset your energetic baseline. All you need to do is release the self-imposed pressure that's been holding you down, so you can rise back to the surface where you truly belong.

I want to share with you a beautiful practice for releasing the limiting beliefs that are blocking your way to feeling good. These three steps have been pivotal for releasing many of the stale beliefs that no longer served me, so I can recalibrate my energy back into alignment with the love of the Universe. Here's how it works.

STEP 1: WITNESS YOUR LIMITING BELIEFS

The first step to eliminating your limiting beliefs is to simply become aware of them.

Take a moment to witness the beliefs that no longer serve you and how they are blocking your happiness. Write it all down in your journal.

Don't beat yourself up over how many limiting beliefs you have. Honor yourself for having the willingness to look within and move forward. It's not about how many limiting beliefs you have, it's about how many limiting beliefs you can release.

Remember, there is no shame in having limiting beliefs. The only shameful thing here is to keep carrying them around like they are some prized possessions.

Many people choose to ignore their limiting beliefs as a way to avoid them. This is why you hear people say things like, "I was born with a negative personality," but these statements are often just excuses that are used to avoid looking at the root cause of their issues.

Remember that beliefs are not set in stone. If you have the ability to pick up a belief, you have the same ability to let go of that belief.

STEP 2: FORGIVE YOURSELF

After you have listed out all your limiting beliefs and how they block your joy. You simply need to forgive yourself for holding on to these limiting beliefs and release them.

Isn't that a bit too simple? Well, that's the point! You are not a forensic investigator, and this is not an episode of *CSI*. Your job is not to dissect the who, what, when, where, how of your limiting beliefs. Because you can't fix something that you didn't cause in the first place. The only thing you are responsible for is holding on to them. So, stop! It really is that simple and profound.

End your forgiveness practice by releasing your limiting beliefs into the hands of the Universe by saying this prayer, "Thank you, Universe, for helping me witness these limiting beliefs that are no longer serving me. I forgive myself for holding on to them and I choose to be free now."

STEP 3: RECALIBRATE YOUR ENERGY

To complete the final step in restoring your natural feel-good state, you will need to drop into meditation.

We've already done a mini-meditation session in our thought experiment in Chapter 1, but we're going to do it for real this time.

Meditation is an important practice for restoring your energetic set point because it allows you to clear your mind of all thoughts by focusing on your breath. When your sole focus is on your breath, you can find relief from the limiting beliefs that are holding your energy down.

Here's how you practice meditation:

- Find a quiet room and sit comfortably in a chair or cross-legged on the floor.
- Close your eyes and take ten deep breaths in and out through your nose.
- Restore the pace of your breathing to normal and direct your attention to the part of your body that feels the breath most strongly. This may be your nostrils, your lips, or your stomach.
- Continue to breathe for at least five minutes.
- If you notice any random thoughts come up during your meditation, simply witness them and say to yourself—*thoughts*. This technique, also known as *labeling*, is a gen-

tle but effective way to bring your attention back to your breath.

- At the end of your meditation, take a moment to notice how you feel. Some people may feel calmer, while others may feel less stressed. For me, I feel a sense of inner peace that is like no other feeling in the world. Notice how all of these emotions are feelings that make you feel good.

The time you spend in meditation is a taste of what it's like to live in your natural state of feeling good. Every time you go into this feel-good state, you heighten your ability to detect thoughts, feelings, and emotions that drain your energy. As you continue to make meditation a habit, it will become easier and easier for you to detect and disengage from negative energy so you can be in this feel-good state all the time.

IT'S TIME TO LET THE FUN BEGIN

You've done great work over the last two chapters. You have now learned two ways to recalibrate your energy back into alignment with feeling good. I decided to give you these tools at the beginning of the book because they will prepare you for the manifestation techniques that are to come. Always remember that you manifest what you feel, not what you do. In order to attract good, you must feel good. And these two chapters are designed to do just that.

Now that you have the tools to restore your energetic state and realign with the love of the Universe, you are more than ready to dive into the Law of Attraction and use it to manifest everything you desire and more. Flip the page and let the fun begin!

CHAPTER 3: THE LAW OF ATTRACTION

Have you ever woken up in a bad mood and noticed that your day just kept getting worse and worse? I certainly have! Let me tell you about this crazy day at work I had a few years ago. My team was having an off-site workday at the corporate office, but I was feeling bummed out because my favorite co-worker called in sick that day. That morning, I was so late to work because I got caught in a crazy traffic jam and proceeded to get lost in the train station. Later when we were heading out for lunch, I walked right into a glass door and bruised my nose. After lunch, emergency requests kept flooding my inbox, so I had to stay later than usual. And then to top it all off, I got a big fat traffic ticket from a cop because all I wanted to do at that point was to get home quickly and get this terrible day over with. This is what people often call a downward spiral. It's almost like the way you feel (or your energetic state) at the start of the day determines the events that will unfold during the rest of the day. At the time, I could not understand why I had such a bad day. But looking back at it now, I can see it was just an example of the Law of Attraction in action.

It is not merely a coincidence that the energy you emit attracts people, situations, and experiences that match it. The Law of Attraction is a universal law that is always at work, regardless of whether you believe in it or not. Like the Law of Gravity, its existence is not determined by whether people know, understand, or believe in it. It's just the way the universe operates. The Law of Attraction is a beautifully designed system that promises great rewards to those who respect it. Not only can you use the Law of Attraction to interrupt the attraction of unwanted experiences, but you can also use it to proactively attract the experiences you desire.

You have two choices when it comes to the Law of Attraction. You can either stick your head in the sand and dismiss your external circumstances as coincidences, or you can try to understand and learn the Law of Attraction so that you can make the most out of it. Many people choose the first option because it feels easier to avoid taking responsibility for your part in attracting these events. But in reality, they are just opening up themselves to attracting more undesirable events in the future. But judging by the fact that you are reading this book, I already know that you are ready and willing to choose the second option. So, let's get started.

THE LAW OF ATTRACTION

The Law of Attraction may seem complicated at first, but it all centers around the basic premise that like attracts like. That which is like onto itself is drawn. This concept is fundamentally applied to energy. But since everything is energy, the scope of this law can be expanded and applied to everything in the universe including objects, people, experiences, thoughts, feelings, and emotions.

The Law of Attraction is the guiding principle behind all physical manifestations of the energy that you emit through your thoughts, feelings, and emotions. The energy you send out determines the type of energy you will receive. This attraction applies to both the things that you want and the things that you don't want. But to truly learn how you can use the Law of Attraction to bring your dreams into reality, you must first understand how energy works on a vibrational level. This brings us to an equally important universal law—the Law of Vibration.

THE LAW OF VIBRATION

As you have learned in Chapter 2, everything in this universe is made up of energy. But the Law of Vibration expands upon this concept by stating that energy is always moving and vibrating. Nothing rests. Everything vibrates at a specific frequency.

Think back to elementary school, when your teacher explained to you the vibrational differences between the various states of water. Water can appear as a solid, liquid, or gas depending on how quickly its atoms vibrate. This is an example of the Law of Vibration in action.

Now take this law and apply it to everything that exists including intangible things like thoughts, feelings, and emotions. Every single thought, feeling, and emotion you have is emitting energy that is vibrating at a certain frequency. This signal of vibrating energy then attracts similar signals of vibrating energy in your vicinity as a result of the Law of Attraction. By achieving absolute vibrational alignment with the energy of your desire, your desire will eventually manifest in the physical form.

The best way to approach the concept of vibration is to think of it as the unit of measure for energy. Just like how we use liters for measuring the volume of a liquid and grams for measuring the weight of an object. Vibration is for measuring the frequency of energy you're emitting at any given time. By using vibration to measure the frequency of energy you send out through your thoughts, feelings, and emotions, you now have a consistent way to understand and predict the kinds of outcomes you will attract.

THE UNIVERSE RESPONDS TO YOUR VIBRATION

When you put the two laws together, you have the basic formula of what it takes to manifest what you want. But now it raises the question, *who* is responsible for putting the two laws together? Here's where the Universe comes into play. The Universe is always working behind the scenes and using these universal laws to deliver you experiences, circumstances, and outcomes that match the vibration you send out.

Your vibration is your request to the Universe, and the Universe always responds to your vibration. Whatever energy you put out; you will receive. There are no exceptions to the rule. When you're vibrating at a high frequency, the Universe will serve you positive outcomes that match your positive vibration. When you're vibrating at a low frequency, the Universe will serve you negative outcomes that match your negative vibration.

YOUR EMOTIONS ARE YOUR VIBRATIONS

Now you may be wondering how you can tell what your vibration is? Well, I have some good news for you. You do not need to pass a test, pay a monthly subscription fee, or install an app to tell your vibration. Because every one of us all has a built-in barometer of our vibration which is our emotions.

In Chapter 2, you learned that your inner guide is always interpreting whether the energy around you is good or bad. The energy is translated into good or bad feelings and these feelings can be further classified into different emotions. Every emotion that you experience emits a specific frequency of vibration. As long as you are in tune with your emotions, you will always know whether the vibration you are sending out is attracting something you want or something you don't want.

While our inner guide is great at telling us whether the energy around us feels good or bad, it can be difficult to shift our emotions from feeling terrible to feeling joyful if we don't know which emotion corresponds to which vibration. This is the perfect opportunity to introduce you to the Emotional Guidance Scale. With the help of this tool, you will have absolute clarity when it comes to determining your vibration.

THE EMOTIONAL GUIDANCE SCALE

The Emotional Guidance Scale is a system developed by Esther Hicks, also known as Abraham-Hicks. Esther Hicks is a world-renowned practitioner of the Law of Attraction. My manifesting practice has been greatly influenced by her work, so I am happy to reference this particular teaching in my book.

The Emotional Guidance Scale is a scale of emotions and their corresponding vibrational frequencies, in sequence from emotions with the highest frequencies of vibration to emotions with the lowest frequencies of vibration. It is broken down into 22 levels of the most commonly felt emotions from joy, love, and appreciation to doubt, anger, and fear.

1. Joy/Knowledge/Empowerment/Freedom/Love/Appreciation
2. Passion
3. Enthusiasm/Eagerness/Happiness
4. Positive Expectation/Belief
5. Optimism
6. Hopefulness
7. Contentment
8. Boredom
9. Pessimism
10. Frustration/Irritation/Impatience
11. "Overwhelment"
12. Disappointment
13. Doubt
14. Worry
15. Blame
16. Discouragement
17. Anger
18. Revenge
19. Hatred/Rage
20. Jealousy
21. Insecurity/Guilt/Unworthiness
22. Fear/Grief/Depression/Despair/Powerlessness

The purpose of this scale is to help you pinpoint exactly where you are on the scale, so you can reach for the next best feeling thought and move up the scale to an emotion with a higher vibration. Instead of being stuck in an emotion with low vibration, the Emotional Guidance Scale gives you an action plan toward where you want to go and the small shifts you can make in order to move to an emotion with a higher vibration.

When you want to raise your vibration, you can simply identify where you are on the Emotional Guidance Scale and reach for better-feeling thoughts that lead to an emotion with a higher vibration. Once you're feeling stable in a new emotion, you've successfully moved up the scale and raised your vibration. The goal is for you to continue the practice of reaching for better-feeling thoughts and slowly make your way back to the top of the scale.

I would encourage you to take this new tool with you and revisit the methods you have learned in the previous chapters. The Emotional Guidance Scale is designed to enhance these practices by giving you the next best feeling emotion to aim for when shifting your thoughts. For example, let's say you are stuck in anger and you want to increase your vibration using Chapter 1's Three Steps to Feeling Good. You may find it difficult to leap directly from anger to love, but with the help of the Emotional Guidance Scale, you can make more manageable shifts to an emotion with slightly higher vibration such as discouragement or blame. Every time you move up the scale, you raise your vibration, and thus, the outcomes you attract.

USING THE LAW OF ATTRACTION CORRECTLY

A common pitfall for new students of the Law of Attraction is to get hooked into the mentality of wanting to use it to control everything in their lives. But the moment you embody this controlling mentality, your vibration plummets and you create resistance against the things you desire. Ultimately, the desire to control is a limiting belief that stems from fear. The fear that we live in a world of scarcity. The fear that if we don't get as much as we can, someone will take it instead. The fear that we can't feel happy or complete until we get exactly what we want.

But instead of seeing the Law of Attraction as a way to control, you can choose to see it as a system that helps you make sense of the circumstances that you are in, reorganize your perspective, and determine the next best action for moving forward. Instead of letting an obstacle in life take down your vibration and cause a downward spiral of events, you know that your next best move is to reach for a better-feeling emotion, raise your vibration, so you can attract more positive people, events, and outcomes that will help you overcome that obstacle and get back on track toward your goals and dreams.

THE TRUE PURPOSE OF THE LAW OF ATTRACTION

The best way to shift away from the controlling mentality is to step back and realize that there is a greater purpose behind the Law of Attraction. The true purpose of the Law of Attraction is to give you a greater understanding of vibration and to use this precise knowledge to realign with the love of the Universe. The Law of Attraction is a powerful tool designed to help you make sense of the circumstances that you are in, reorganize your vibration, and plan your next steps so that you can make your way back into alignment with the Universe.

Let's do a quick recap of all of the tools the Universe has given us to use in this physical realm. We have our inner guide that translates energy into feelings, our innate desire to feel good, our emotions which are absolute indicators of our vibration, our ability to witness negative thoughts, our ability to choose better-feeling thoughts, and universal laws such as the Law of Attraction and the Law of Vibration. Each of these tools helps us survive in the physical world, but the combination of these tools serves a greater purpose, which is to help us align with the Universe. Most people go a lifetime without learning how to use them, but those who are spiritually awakened can see that these tools are the Universe's open invitation for co-creation.

The Universe is an all-encompassing, ever-present, force of love. Looking at the Emotional Guidance Scale, you will see that love is at the top of the scale, which means it is the energy with the highest vibration possible. So, if you want to align with the Universe, all you have to do is simply align with love. No matter what emotion you are feeling, the Emotional Guidance Scale gives you the precise roadmap of vibrational shifts you need to make in order to come back to love.

When you align with the energy of love, you are in absolute alignment with the Universe. In this state of vibrational harmony, you are no longer separate from the Universe. You become one with the Universe. This spiritual union is the beginning of a lifelong collaborative relationship with the Universe to manifest a life beyond your wildest dreams. In Chapter 4, I will reveal to you the true meaning of manifestation and a practical method for manifesting solutions of the highest good for all.

CHAPTER 4: MANIFESTING

Now that you have learned about the Law of Attraction and how it works on a vibrational level, it's finally time to learn how you can use it to manifest what you want. You may have heard of people manifesting what they want by creating vision boards, writing affirmations in a journal, or meditating every day. These are all activities that can help you manifest your desires by raising your vibration, but it is crucial to understand the three main components of the manifestation process before getting into the nitty-gritty details. Many of us grew up with the limiting belief that we must work hard in order to "make it happen", but true manifestation is quite the opposite of that. It all comes down to three main steps: Ask, Believe, and Receive.

ASK

The first step to manifesting is to simply ask the Universe for what you want. As you have learned in Chapter 3, the Universe responds to vibration. Therefore, the way you ask for what you want is through the vibration you emit through your thoughts, feelings, and emotions instead of your words. Every thought, feeling, and emotion that you experience is a vibrational transmission to the Universe asking for what you want.

The Universe is always saying *yes* to your vibration. When you think about something that you want, you're asking the Universe for it. When you think about something that you don't want, you're asking the Universe for it. But from our experiment in Chapter 1, we know that most of the thoughts that we have are involuntary. So, it can be challenging to manage your vibrational requests to the Universe by monitoring your thoughts.

But since every thought evokes a specific feeling, there's a better way to gauge whether your vibrational requests are in alignment with your desires or not. The best way to know if you are asking for something that you want is through how you feel. Your feelings always tell you whether you are asking for something that you want or something that you don't want. When your ask is aligned with the truth of who you are, you feel good. When your ask is out of alignment with the truth of who you are, you feel bad. This is why feeling good is always the perfect indicator that you are on track to manifesting what you want.

BELIEVE

The second step to manifesting is super easy because it doesn't require any work on your part. All it takes is your willingness to believe that the Universe is constantly responding to the energy you send out and bringing you people, experiences, and outcomes that match your vibration. Every single vibrational request is fully received and responded to immediately.

The Universe created the Law of Attraction so that we can have a consistent formula to ask for what we want. As such, the Universe respects the Law of Attraction and it is impartial when it comes to responding to our vibrations. When you send out high vibrational energy, you will receive high vibrational outcomes. When you send out low vibrational energy, you will receive low vibrational outcomes. There are no exceptions.

RECEIVE

The final step to manifesting is to receive what you have asked for through vibrational alignment. In order to receive what the Universe has in store for you, you need to align your vibration with the vibration of your desire. In other words, you must think and feel as if your desire has already manifested. By assuming the energy of a future manifestation in the present moment, you are bringing yourself into vibrational alignment with your desire. Once you are in alignment with what you want, you will need to maintain your high vibrational energy in order to allow your desire to manifest in its physical form.

The receiving process is kind of like downloading a large file from the internet. When you achieve vibrational alignment with your desire, the downloading begins. But if you want to actually *use* the file, you must maintain this vibrational alignment until the download is fully completed. In other words, you must sustain your vibrational alignment over a period of time before your desire can manifest in its physical form. This period of time is what is more commonly known as the buffer of time.

THE BUFFER OF TIME

The buffer of time is the time gap between the asking of your desire and the receiving of the physical manifestation of your desire. The buffer of time is the reason why the receiving process is viewed as one of the most challenging steps in the manifestation process. It's the one part of manifesting that trips most people up. More often than not, our impatience gets the best of us. We're so used to getting things instantly, that the need to wait for our desires to manifest can cause individuals to spiral down into emotions with low vibration such as doubt or worry. The moment you slip into low vibration, you fall out of alignment with your desires, and thus the receiving process is interrupted.

Instead of seeing the buffer of time as a hurdle to manifesting, I actually see it as a blessing. If we instantly receive everything we ask for, the world would be in such a mess! Think about the flip side of things and apply the buffer of time to the manifestation of the things that you don't want. Even though I'm on a spiritual path, I still get hooked into fear-based thoughts once in a while. Without the buffer of time, my unintentional detour into fear will instantly manifest people, situations, and outcomes that I don't want.

The buffer of time is here to stay, so you should learn to use it to your advantage. Know that manifestation is a process that will require you to maintain your high vibration and make feeling good your highest priority. Whenever you notice your impatience starts to kick in, simply remind yourself that it's not that your manifestation didn't come. It's just that your manifestation hasn't come yet.

MANIFESTING IS MORE THAN JUST THE LAW OF ATTRACTION

Contrary to popular beliefs, manifesting is actually a different practice from the Law of Attraction. While the manifestation process draws on the concepts of the Law of Attraction, it is ultimately a spiritual practice.

Having faith in a higher power is the key to effortless manifestations. Yes, you can attract what you want by following the Law of Attraction principles, but that would involve constant monitoring of your thoughts, feelings, and emotions. But why would you want to do that when you can simply align with love and allow everything you need to flow to you?

A SPIRITUAL APPROACH TO MANIFESTING

The best way to approach manifestation is to treat it as a collaboration with the Universe. When most people learn about the Law of Attraction for the first time, they become engrossed in the processes, the actions, and the doing. Instead of perceiving it as a way to co-create what they want with the Universe, manifestation becomes a manic solo performance. In trying to control the manifestation, they lose sight of the most important requirement for manifesting—which is to feel good.

Spirituality and manifestation go hand in hand. Every single step of the manifestation process benefits when you remain committed to feeling good by listening to your inner guidance system. Your job is not to force the manifestations to happen, but to align with the Universe through feeling good, and simply allow the manifestations to come to you as you cultivate your spiritual connection. The most beautiful and effortless manifestations do not come through force but through spiritual surrender and unwavering faith in the Universe.

THE TRUE MEANING OF MANIFESTING

I want to share with you the spiritual definition of manifesting. This definition of manifesting transformed the way I approach manifestation and it comes from a quote from one of my favorite spiritual teachers, Gabrielle Bernstein.

"Manifesting is the creative process of aligning with the energy of the Universe to co-create an experience that elevates your spirit and the spirit of the world."

This one sentence contains five truths that will shape the way you manifest forever.

1. **Manifesting Is A Creative Process**: The word *creative* is used here because manifesting requires you to accept a new way of thinking. You must be willing to shed old limiting beliefs and think outside the box if you want to manifest intentionally.
2. **Alignment Is Imperative**: You have to align with the energy of the Universe before you can co-create with the Universe. Raising your vibration to match the loving vibration of the Universe is a prerequisite to manifesting.
3. **It Takes Two To Co-Create**: Manifesting is a collaboration between you and the Universe. It's not a genie lamp situation where you can sit back and watch it happen. You must be willing to do your part if you want to manifest your desires.

4. **The Goal Is To Feel Good**: The goal of manifesting is not just to get what you want, but to use the co-creation experience to feel good and become an even closer vibrational match to love.
5. **Go Beyond Yourself**: Make it your mission to manifest things that not only benefit yourself but also the rest of the world. Being of service to others is the best way to raise your vibration and manifest even more miracles. True manifesting is not just about manifesting solutions for you, it's about manifesting solutions of the highest good for all.

When I first read this message, I was shocked at how one simple sentence can contain so many truths. To this day, these five principles still serve as the foundation of my manifestation practice. In fact, they inspired me to create my Spiritual Manifestation Method.

SPIRITUAL MANIFESTATION METHOD

I'm so excited to share with you my Spiritual Manifestation Method. During my spiritual journey, I have tried a myriad of techniques for manifesting, but I always end up coming back to these five steps.

The Spiritual Manifestation Method expands on the Ask, Believe, and Receive framework by providing a concrete step-by-step guide that you can follow along with. These steps are designed to be simple and practical. This method is perfect for new seekers who want to get into manifesting, but it can also serve as the foundation for experienced manifestors to build upon and incorporate their own practices as they co-create with the Universe. Here is how the Spiritual Manifestation Method works.

STEP 1: BE SPECIFIC ABOUT WHAT YOU WANT

The first step to manifesting is to be specific about what you want.

Put your pen to paper and write down exactly what you want to manifest.

Describe it in detail and be as specific as possible. This step is your opportunity to get clear about what you want to manifest so you can work with the Universe to co-create it in your reality.

For example, if you're looking to make a career change. Don't just write in your journal that you want to manifest a new job! Supplement it with details.

Here are some sample questions you should ask yourself so you can get clear on the kind of job you want to manifest:

- What kind of job do you want?
- What will you do there?
- What is your ideal work environment?
- How much does it pay?
- Where is the job located?

Listen to your intuition and answer these questions honestly. What you write down in this step will be used to visualize your desires in a subsequent step. So, take your time to write a thorough answer.

STEP 2: CLARIFY WHY YOU WANT IT

The second step is to clarify the intentions behind your desire. In other words, why do you want to manifest this desire? Write it down in your journal.

The *why* is very important because your intention affects your vibration which determines whether you will attract positive or negative outcomes. Refer to the Emotional Guidance Scale and check the vibrations of the emotions that are supporting your desire.

Going back to the earlier example, do you want to manifest a new job because you want to do something that you love? Or do you want to manifest a new job so you can prove your worth to your parents?

Both requests are asking the Universe for the same thing (a new job), but they are backed by very different intentions. One is backed by high vibrational energy such as love and passion. The other is backed by low vibrational energy such as insecurity and unworthiness.

As a result, the outcomes you receive will be vastly different. Remember the like attracts like principle, the outcomes you receive will always match whatever energy you send out into the Universe.

This step is your opportunity to get honest about the intention behind your desire so that you can support it with more positive energy. If you notice your request is currently backed by negative energy, simply forgive yourself and come back to it. Use any of the practices in this book to shift your vibration and try this step again when you're ready.

One way to supercharge the positive energy behind your request to the Universe is to think beyond yourself by considering how your manifestation will elevate those around you. A manifestation that is backed by love and service is one of the most positive vibrations you can send to the Universe, and in return, you'll receive an equally positive outcome.

STEP 3: FEEL THE GOOD FEELINGS

Once you have clarity on what you want to manifest and the positive intention behind it. Your job is to align yourself with the good vibration of the manifestation in order to receive it.

Your energy creates your reality. Therefore, it's important to remember that it's the *feeling* that attracts when it comes to manifestation.

One of the best ways to get into the feeling of what it's like to experience your manifestation is through visualization.

Visualization may seem like an intimidating practice but it's likely something that you do every day. When you're planning out your day ahead, you're visualizing. When you're thinking about your upcoming weekend, you're visualizing. When you're picturing how your dinner date will go, you're visualizing. The only difference here is you will be intentionally visualizing your manifestation and the good feelings it brings you.

Visualization is so powerful because it allows you to assume the vibrational energy of a future manifestation *as if* you are experiencing it in the present moment. Once you are in vibrational alignment with your desire, you are in the perfect position to receive your manifestation.

- To get started, bring your journal to a quiet place where you will not be disturbed for a while.
- Get into a comfortable seated position and read what you have written in the previous steps. Read it over a few times so you know it by heart.
- Then close your eyes and direct your focus to your breathing. Take slow and steady breaths and start to imagine your manifestation as if it has already come true.
- First, you should focus on the specific description of the manifestation you wrote down in Step 1. Use your five senses to paint the most realistic mental image of the manifestation.
- Once you have a clear mental image of the manifestation, shift your focus away from the physical description of it, and direct your attention to the good feelings it brings you.
- Recall your positive intentions behind your desire and feel the high-vibe emotions that this manifestation brings you. You may feel excited, optimistic, or happy which are all emotions with high vibrations.
- Expand your visualization to include your loved ones and imagine how the manifestation will elevate their energy.

Continue to visualize for 5 to 10 minutes. There are no time requirements when it comes to visualization. If you find that this process brings you joy or even a smile to your face, you can trust that you are in absolute alignment with your desire.

STEP 4: TAKE INSPIRED ACTION

Manifesting is a process of co-creation, which means it's a collaborative process. You must be willing to work with the Universe in order to bring your manifestation into reality, and this involves taking action. Not just any action, but *inspired* action.

Inspired actions are effortless, confident, and fun. There is no doubt or hesitation, and everything just flows. You are not taking these actions because you *need* to but because you *want* to. You are so certain in the outcome that you are inspired to take action in order to get closer to your manifestation.

There's no big or small when it comes to taking action. Whether it is a simple google search on how to start your own business or delivering a sales pitch to a new client. You just need to take action from a place of spiritual alignment—a place that feels good.

If you have trouble grasping the idea of taking inspired action, simply think about how you approach your favorite hobby or pastime. You do it out of sheer enjoyment. You do it because it feels good. You do it because it brings you joy. There is no pressure, no expectations, and no need to control the outcome. Apply this same energy when you're taking action toward your manifestation, and the results will be astonishing.

If you ever find yourself getting hooked into negative or low-vibe energy, feel free to revisit the first three steps to realign your vibration. Actions that are taken from a place of alignment will produce much greater outcomes, compared to actions that are taken from a place of misalignment.

STEP 5: LET GO AND ALLOW

The final step is to let go and allow the manifestation to come into your reality. This is the process of receiving your manifestation by maintaining the high vibrational energy you cultivated in the previous steps.

Overcoming the buffer of time will be a real test for many people. Many novice manifestors mess up at this stage because they are constantly checking and worrying about whether their desire will manifest or not. This is a big no-no because it essentially negates all the work you have done to get into a place of alignment. The emotion of worry is low-vibration energy according to the Emotional Guidance Scale, so it lowers your vibration and throws you out of alignment with your desire.

The biggest lesson here is to be patient and trust that the Universe has your back. When you have faith in the plan of the Universe, it makes it easy to let go of the outcome. Even though what you want may not manifest as quickly as you hope or in the same way that you expect. Trust that the Universe's plan always exceeds yours and know that it is of the highest good for all.

Use this prayer to surrender the outcomes of your manifestations, "Universe, I surrender my timelines, agenda, and desires to you. I trust that you are leading me toward solutions of the highest good for all. I step back and let you lead the way. Thank you."

MANIFESTATION IS THE RESULT OF FEELING GOOD

Remember that manifestation is the result of feeling good, not the reverse. Many people live from achievement to achievement because they are under the limiting belief that "When I get this, I'll be happy," or "When I manifest this, I will feel good."

But the secret to manifesting is to feel good right now, so that you can get into co-creation with the Universe. You must be happy with what you have right now before you can reach for more.

This truth was why I felt compelled to title this book *Feeling Good*. Feeling good in the present moment is the fundamental requirement behind all manifestations. And the Universe has generously equipped us with an abundance of tools so that we could guide ourselves back to feeling good. Such as our ability to feel and shift our energy, our inner guide who always leads us toward what feels good, our ability to form a spiritual relationship with a God of our own understanding. All these innate abilities are there for a reason. They are there to guide us back into alignment with the truth of who we are so that we can ask, believe, and receive everything we desire.

If you want to manifest what you want, you must commit to the practice of feeling good. The moment you claim feeling good as your birthright, you reclaim the ability to manifest everything you want and more.

CHAPTER 5: RAISE YOUR VIBRATION

Now that you understand the importance of keeping your vibration high in order to receive your manifestation, it's time for me to introduce you to some practices you can do to proactively raise your vibration.

This entire chapter is dedicated to practices that you can use on a daily basis to shift your energy and raise your vibration. Some activities will come naturally to you, or you may experience resistance to others. If you find yourself gravitating toward a certain practice more than others, I want to reassure you that it is perfectly normal. In fact, that is a very good sign that you are in tune with your inner guidance system. Trust that your preferences are simply your inner guide's way of leading you toward the practices that are best suited for you. The only thing that matters here is you enjoy the practice, and it makes you feel good.

Throughout my deep dive into manifestation, I have tried out countless practices and activities with the goal of raising my vibration. Out of the many practices I've tried, meditation was one of those activities that I found the most challenging. The concept of meditation was not new to me, but I've never been keen on practicing it on a daily basis. Because of my busy schedule, I felt stressed out whenever I had to do a meditation. Nevertheless, I was determined to practice meditation because it seemed to be the core practice that all spiritual teachers rave about.

I began to push myself to sit through longer and longer sessions of meditation. Instead of listening to my inner guide, I tried to force myself to enjoy it. I was stuck in the limiting belief that I needed to do rigorous meditation sessions because everyone else did it. In doing so, I lost sight of the most important aspect of which was to feel good.

When I recognized how this limiting belief was affecting me, I turned to the Universe for guidance. I said this prayer, "Thank you, Universe, for helping me see past my limiting beliefs. I am ready to realign with my truth which is to feel good." The moment I called out this limiting belief was the moment I found release from the need for comparison. Now I approach meditation with a much more relaxed mindset. I realized the success of a meditation practice does not depend on how long you sit in stillness, but how good it feels when you sit in stillness.

Let this be a lesson for you to never lose sight of the need to feel good when raising your vibration. Ease into each practice with a mindset of having fun. Release all expectations and simply let your inner guide lead you toward a practice that resonates with you. Once you're feeling comfortable with the practice, feel free to customize it, and make it your own. There are no wrong paths here as long as you feel good.

APPRECIATION

Appreciation is a simple but powerful practice for raising your vibration. Referring back to the Emotional Guidance Scale, you will see that appreciation is at the top of the scale, which means it is one of the emotions with the highest vibration you can feel.

When you express appreciation, you shift your attention away from the areas in your life that are lacking and toward the areas that are thriving. In doing so, you pivot your energetic momentum and catapult your vibration all the way to the top of the Emotional Guidance Scale.

What I love about appreciation is that it is accessible and available to you at all times. You can appreciate your job during your morning commute. You can appreciate your loved ones while you're cooking a meal. You can appreciate your abundance while shopping for a gift. All that is required is a willingness to shift your perspective from lack to abundance.

The most important rule you need to remember when practicing appreciation is you must feel the good feelings it brings you. It's not just about going through the motions of saying or writing down what you're grateful for that day. Shift your focus away from the physical action of appreciation and toward the feelings of appreciation.

Another way to approach appreciation is to think of it as a mini visualization exercise. Start by focusing your attention on the object or person of your appreciation. Once you have a good mental image in your head, direct your attention to how good that object or person makes you feel. Think about what they do for you and what you can do for them. Dwell in this feeling of appreciation to raise your vibration. The goal is to assume the feelings of appreciation in the present moment so you can shift your energy upward.

If you want to take your appreciation game to the next level, you can show your appreciation for others by being of service to them. Make this quote by Aung San Suu Kyi your mantra, "When you're feeling helpless, help someone." Serving others without expecting anything in return is the literal embodiment of unconditional love. And when you are aligned with love, you are in alignment with the Universe.

JOURNAL

Journaling is another great way to raise your vibration and bring your manifestations into reality. You may notice that many of the practices in this book involve a journal and a pen and that is for a reason. Your words are powerful and writing them down is a sign of your commitment to your spiritual practice. When you put pen to paper, it's a massive statement to the Universe that you are ready to realign and shift your energy. I have had great success with journaling, and I have used it to manifest many miracles in my life.

There are no rules when it comes to journaling. The only goal is to have fun and feel good when you are writing in your journal. Although the content of my journal is different every day, there are three topics that I always cover. If you have never tried journaling before, I would encourage you to use these points as a framework for getting started.

1. **How Was Your Day:** What did you manifest today? What were some of the miracles that occurred? What were some small wins? What were the lessons?
2. **What Are You Grateful For:** What are you grateful for today? Who are you grateful for today? Why are you grateful for them?
3. **What Do You Want to Manifest:** What do you want to manifest? Why do you want to manifest it? How does this manifestation elevate your energy and the energy of those around you?

After you have finished your journal entry for the day. Take a moment to read over what you wrote and bask in the good feelings it brings you. Don't skip this part. Meditating on what you have written down is the most important part of your journaling practice because it allows you to assume the positive energy of your words in the present moment.

The most common mistake when journaling is to use it as a place to vent about your life. Although you may think that you're doing other people a favor by directing your negativity into your journal, you're actually doing yourself a great disservice vibrationally.

Take the example of my friend, Emma. We were having a chat and the topic of journaling came up. We eagerly shared our journaling practice, but she revealed to me she was having trouble with it. This piqued my interest, so we proceeded to share what we would usually write in our journals. Even though we both wrote in our journals daily, the content that we wrote about was vastly different.

While I used my journal as a place to reflect on my day, she used her journal as a place to vent. It was full of negative stories about the day and how bad they made her feel. It's no wonder she felt discouraged by her journaling practice. When you write about negativity, you assume the negative emotions you felt in the past and bring them into the present moment. By reliving the negative vibrations in the present, you are vulnerable to manifesting even more negative outcomes in the future.

Let my friend's story be a warning for you about the power of your words. When you are writing in your journal, you are focusing your vibration on certain thoughts and feelings. And the Universe is always saying *yes* to your vibration. Make your journal a happy place and watch as miracles unfold before you.

YOGA

I would like to preface this by saying that I am not a yoga instructor and I do not claim to be a yogi by any means. But there's one thing that I do know which is my love for yoga. Besides the obvious health benefits, what I love the most about yoga is the meaning behind it.

The word *yoga* is derived from the Sanskrit word *yuj*, which means to join or to unite. According to Yogic scriptures, the purpose of yoga is to unite the consciousness of the individual with the consciousness of the Universe. In other words, the goal of yoga is to align with the Universe physically, mentally, and spiritually. And as you now know, alignment with the Universe is the key to manifesting.

A common misconception about yoga is that it requires you to be very flexible in order to pull off those intricate poses. But yoga is not just a fitness regiment, it's a spiritual practice for you to honor your body, connect with your inner guide, and realign with the Universe.

Don't let the complicated poses intimidate you from developing your yoga practice. In fact, one of the most powerful yoga poses, *Shavasana*, simply requires you to lie down on the floor with your arms by your sides and legs shoulder-width apart and focus on your breathing.

You don't need an expensive yoga studio membership to practice yoga. You don't even need a fancy yoga mat or yoga pants to get started. A yoga sequence I recommend to everyone is the *Sun Salutation*. This yoga sequence is easy and approachable for beginners, but it can also be customized and built upon by seasoned yogis. Remember that raising your vibration is all about having fun. All it takes is a willingness to try and a commitment to feel good.

AFFIRMATIONS

The final practice I want to introduce you to is affirmations. Simply put, affirmations are positive statements that can help you challenge and replace negative thoughts. Assuming the positive feelings behind an affirmation is a powerful way to shift your energy and raise your vibration. Affirmations hold a special place in my heart because it's the practice that resonates with me the most. Affirmations have the ability to lift you up when you're feeling low and elevate you when you're thriving.

But affirmations are more than just empty words. The number one thing to remember when using affirmations is that it's all about how they make you feel. Affirmations only work when you *believe* in what you are saying. Don't recite affirmations just for the sake of doing it. Choose a few that resonate with you and imagine how good it feels to live out the affirmations. If reciting an affirmation brings you a sense of relief, then you are on the right track to mastering the power of affirmations.

Another way to view affirmations is to treat them like short prayers to the Universe. When you say an affirmation out loud, you are not just saying it to yourself. Your affirmation is also a massive statement to the Universe that you are ready to seek spiritual solutions. Instead of relying on your own strength, use affirmations to rearrange your perspective so you can receive loving guidance from the Universe.

NOT ALL AFFIRMATIONS ARE CREATED EQUAL

A common mistake I see people make with affirmations is choosing an affirmation that doesn't work well for them. Most of the time, it's not that affirmations don't work, it's just that the affirmation you're using doesn't work for you.

To be effective at raising your vibration, the affirmation needs to be specific and backed by positive energy. For instance, if you are trying to manifest financial abundance. An affirmation like, "I need more money," will not be as effective as, "I feel blessed by the abundance that is all around me."

If you want to get into the practice of affirmations, I highly recommend you try writing your own affirmations. The most powerful affirmations are the affirmations you write for yourself because no one knows you and your circumstances better than *you*. This is why the affirmations you create yourself will resonate much more compared to generic ones made by someone else. Here are five tips you can follow to write your own affirmations.

TIP 1: FOCUS ON YOURSELF

Affirmations should revolve around *you*. The way other people act or behave is outside of your control. You are only responsible for your own thoughts, feelings, and emotions.

That's why it's helpful to start with an "I am..." statement.

For example, if you want to get a promotion, don't write an affirmation such as, "My boss will give me a promotion soon." Remember, the goal of affirmations is not to control other people's actions.

Reframe the affirmation from your own perspective such as, "I am open to receiving new career opportunities."

TIP 2: WRITE IN THE PRESENT TENSE

The main purpose of affirmations is to raise your vibration. And the only way you can assume a higher vibration in the present moment is to feel as if it is already true. This is why it's important to write using the present tense as if the affirmation is happening right now.

Avoid writing in the future tense by using phrases such as, "I will..." or "I am going to..." These phrases imply that the affirmation has not yet happened which prevents you from feeling the good vibes of the affirmation.

For example, if you want to get out of debt, don't write an affirmation such as, "I am going to be debt-free soon."

Reframe the affirmation to focus on the present moment such as, "It feels so good to be free from debt."

TIP 3: BE POSITIVE

Always frame your affirmations from a positive perspective.

Avoid using negations such as *not, don't, won't,* and *can't.* We often use these words when we don't want something to happen. But according to the Law of Attraction, even when you focus on the absence of something, you're still giving attention to it, and thus attracting it into your reality.

For example, if you want to have clear skin, don't write an affirmation such as, "I don't want to get acne." Guess what happens when you remove the word don't? The affirmation actually says, "I want to get acne!"

Instead of focusing on what you *don't* want, your affirmation should focus on what you *do* want.

Reframe the statement to affirm what you desire, "I feel safe knowing that my skin can heal itself."

TIP 4: FOCUS ON HOW YOU FEEL

When you're writing affirmations, put the emphasis on how you want to feel instead of specific outcomes.

As you have learned in the previous chapters, you manifest what you feel, not what you want. So, make it your goal to use affirmations to raise your vibration.

For example, if you want to manifest a fit body, don't write an affirmation such as, "I want to look fit and toned."

Reframe that affirmation to focus on how you want to feel by saying, "It feels great to live in a healthy body."

TIP 5: MAKE YOUR AFFIRMATIONS BELIEVABLE

The final and most important tip for writing your own affirmations is to make them believable. Because the key to getting the most out of affirmations is to actually believe in them.

If your affirmations are so unrealistic that you have trouble believing in them, they will just feel false which can potentially leave you feeling even worse than before.

A good way to make your affirmations more believable is to tweak them using gentle phrases such as, "I am willing to..." or "I choose to..."

For example, if you are feeling depressed, an affirmation like, "I am happy," will feel out of reach. According to the Emotional Guidance Scale, there's a big vibrational variance between depression and happiness, so it can be difficult to leap from depression to happiness in one step.

But you can reframe the affirmation to a more realistic statement such as, "I am willing to choose better-feeling thoughts."

It's often the simplest shifts that make the biggest differences when it comes to affirmations.

THE KEY TO RAISING YOUR VIBRATION

Throughout this chapter, you may have noticed that I placed heavy emphasis on feeling the positive energy that these practices bring to you. It doesn't matter which activity you do or how well you do it. What matters is you must simply feel good while doing it. When you assume the energy of feeling good in the present moment, you shift your energy and raise your vibration.

Just like how everyone has their preferences when it comes

to likes and dislikes. You will most likely gravitate toward one practice over another. Some people may prefer to do yoga, while others may prefer to journal. Simply listen to your inner guide and commit to the practice that best resonates with you. Make your favorite practice a daily habit, so you can use it to realign with the Universe and get into the co-creation of your desires.

Now that you have learned how to raise your vibration, you will also need to equip yourself with a few ways to protect the good energy you have cultivated. As you go through life, you will encounter people, situations, and circumstances that will challenge your vibration. You can either allow these situations to take down your vibration or you can protect your energy and use these moments as opportunities to get closer into alignment with the loving presence of the Universe. In the following chapter, I will give you some practical methods you can use to protect your vibration.

CHAPTER 6: PROTECT YOUR VIBRATION

What's the most important thing in your life? Some of you may say family. While others may say health. There is no right or wrong answer here, it's simply a matter of priorities. But one thing that most people forget to prioritize is their energy. Life can give you a million reasons to lower your vibration, and you can quickly end up with an empty energy tank if you are not careful with how you spend your energy. This is one of the reasons why so many people feel they have no control over their lives. When you let your external circumstances determine your vibration, you send out mixed vibrational signals to the Universe and manifest things that you don't necessarily want.

Many of us spend the majority of our lives offering vibrations in response to the environments, situations, and circumstances that we are currently facing. When something good happens in our lives, we feel good and emit high vibrations. But when something bad happens in our lives, we feel bad and emit low vibrations. I'm sure you can start to see how this can become problematic. If you let your external reality determine your vibration, you basically give up your manifestation power. Why let your circumstances determine your vibration when you can determine your circumstances using your vibration?

When you begin to prioritize your vibration and perceive the world from the lens of energy, you will experience a seismic shift in your ability to manifest what you want. By choosing to perceive my day-to-day moments from the perspective of energy, I have experienced a radical transformation in my happiness, joy, and more importantly, my spiritual connection to a higher power. There's a reason why the Universe responds to energy instead of words. Words can easily be twisted or misinterpreted, but energy never lies. When you practice seeing the world in terms of energy, you can experience the world through the eyes of the God within you. In other words, you become one with the Universe.

Before I introduce you to the methods you can use to protect your vibration, I want to reassure you that prioritizing your good vibration is not a *selfish* act, but a *selfless* one. Every time you choose to respectfully walk away from a negative situation, you not only protect your own energy, but also the energy of those around you. By respecting the importance of energetic vibration, you are being of high service to those around you. Treat your energy like a bank account and remember that you can't give with an empty wallet.

CHECK IN WITH YOURSELF

An average person thinks over 60,000 thoughts a day. That's a lot of thoughts to keep track of! Let alone trying to choose the best thoughts in order to manifest what we want. But the good thing is we have a better and simpler way of knowing if we are vibrationally aligned with our desires which is through our feelings. Your inner guide is always informing you whether you are emitting positive or negative energy through your feelings, but it is up to you whether to follow or resist this guidance.

If you are someone who is not used to being in touch with your emotions, set a few alarms on your smartphone to remind you to check in with yourself, and see how you are feeling throughout the day. If you are feeling good, simply keep doing what you're doing and ride this positive momentum of energy. But if you are feeling bad, take a moment to witness your emotions and use any method in this book to proactively shift to a better feeling. You can say an affirmation. You can use the Emotional Guidance Scale. Or you can even do a quick 5-minute meditation. It doesn't matter what you do, as long as it brings you one step closer to your truth which is to feel good. Negative thoughts can be addicting, but all it takes is a shift in perception to interrupt the downward momentum and reset your vibration.

By establishing this habit of checking in with your feelings, it will soon become second nature to you. It will become natural for you to live in alignment with your inner guide as the Universe has intended. Remember that you were born with this connection to your inner guide. Even when you were a baby, you instinctively knew that your purpose was to feel good and be joyful. This is why it feels so good to live in high vibration because joy is your birthright.

Listening to the voice of your intuition is not something that you have to learn. It is an *unlearning* of the limiting beliefs you picked up along the way. A return to form that's been a long time coming.

SET LOVING BOUNDARIES

In this digital age, where everyone is expected to be available anytime and anywhere, we must set and maintain boundaries to protect our energy. A lot of people are hesitant to set boundaries because they are under the limiting belief that it is unkind or unloving to do so. But boundaries are there to protect not only your energy but also the energy of everyone around you. So, setting boundaries is actually one of the *most* loving things you can do for your loved ones.

Setting boundaries doesn't mean you have to completely cut out certain people from your life or block them on your phone. It can be as simple as gently redirecting a negative conversation to a more positive place or choosing to walk away from a heated argument. When you become conscious of the energetic exchanges that are happening during your day-to-day conversations, you gain the ability to protect your energy and the energy of those around you.

Try saying a silent prayer to your higher power before entering difficult conversations. A simple prayer I always use is, "Thank you, Universe, for protecting my energy. I'm ready to let my inner guide come forward and lead the way." This powerful prayer allows you to hear the guidance from your intuition, the part of you that senses energy, during the upcoming conversation. Trust in your inner guidance system's ability to guide your words and prioritize energy that feels good.

When you feel that a conversation is heading toward negativity, gently redirect the topic of conversation to something else. Taking into account the momentum effect caused by the Law of Attraction, it's best to take action as soon as you notice an energetic shift in the wrong direction. Negative energy attracts more negative energy, so it's easier to interrupt negativity in its infancy before it has a chance to pick up vibrational momentum.

But for those low-vibe conversations that you just can't get out of, make it a rule to enforce your boundaries and respectfully disengage. Protect your vibration by saying, "I'm not comfortable with discussing this topic, and I would appreciate it if we can change the subject," or "I'm not quite ready to share my opinion on this topic yet, can we revisit this at a later date?" Remember that your energy speaks louder than your words. When your assertion is backed by positive intentions, the other party can feel that you're coming from a genuine place. And if they truly care for you and your well-being, they will respect your boundaries and honor your willingness to speak up.

YOU'RE NOT RESPONSIBLE FOR OTHER PEOPLE'S HAPPINESS

When we see our loved ones get stuck in negative cycles of low vibration, it's natural for us to want to reach out and help fix things. But one thing you need to realize is that every single individual is responsible for their own vibrations. Vibrations are emitted through your thoughts, feelings, and emotions and the only one who can truly change your thoughts, feelings, and emotions is *you*.

The good thing is we were all born with a connection to our inner guides. Our intuition is always guiding us toward what feels good, as long as we are willing to listen. Although the connection to this inner guide may be weakened due to life's circumstances, situations, and experiences, the connection can never be severed.

This seemingly difficult time your loved one is going through may actually be the Universe's way of guiding them toward restoring their connection to their inner guide. You probably have heard of the saying, "The good thing about hitting rock bottom is that there's only one way left to go which is up." Rock bottoms may be painful, but they are often powerful moments for spiritual surrender. Just as I hit rock bottom by starving my body in order to feel good, it was the exact situation that led me to stop relying on my own strength and surrender to a higher power.

The lesson here is to simply have faith and trust in the power of our inner guides. Just like how it has intuitively guided you to read this book, this same inner guide is silently at work in everyone's lives. It is not your job to deprive someone of their dark moments. The most loving thing you can do in these situations is to maintain your positive vibration and be a shining example of what it looks like to live a life that is committed to feeling good.

FREE YOURSELF WITH THE F WORD

Use the "F-word" liberally and say it like you really mean it. No, I'm not talking about the "F-word" that rhymes with duck. The "F-word" I'm referring to here is *forgiveness*. Forgiveness is the ultimate tool for dissolving negative energy and protecting your vibration.

Forgiveness is not really about letting go of what other people have done to you, but it is about releasing yourself from the grasp of resentment, anger, and bitterness, which are all emotions with low vibration.

The moment you forgive is the moment you let yourself off the hook and give yourself permission to feel good again. Holding onto resentment does nothing to those who hurt you; it only harms yourself. When you are stuck in a low vibrational state, you're asking the Universe to manifest more low vibrational outcomes into *your* life—not other people's lives.

An even more important application of the "F-word" is to forgive yourself. As a student on a spiritual path, you will have moments where you detour into fear. You will have days where you feel stuck in low vibration. You will have times when you take action from a place of misalignment rather than faith. But these moments are where the power of self-forgiveness comes in. Forgiveness dissolves the past and allows you to pivot your negative thoughts back to love. Make forgiveness your mantra. Forgive generously and forgive quickly. Forgiveness is the quickest way back to love.

CALL OUT YOUR INNER CRITIC

One of the greatest things we can do to protect our vibrations is to silence the voice of our inner critic, also known as the ego. The ego is the part of you that holds on to fear for a false sense of protection. The ego is the part of you that resists the guidance from your intuition. The ego is the part of you that fails to see beyond the physical realm.

The ego is single-handedly the most ruthless vibration killer known to the human race. The ego permeates our minds with self-destructive thoughts like, "I'm not good enough," or "I am a complete failure," or "I don't deserve to feel good." It's crazy how we would never say these things to someone we love, but the ego does not hold back when the target is ourselves.

The only way to protect yourself is to call out the ego for its nasty behavior. The moment you recognize that you are separate from the ego, you can realign with your inner guide and hear the loving voice of your intuition. Your intuition is always leading you toward what's best for you. It's the north star that points you toward solutions of the highest good. Whenever you get hooked on fear-based thoughts, simply go back to Chapter 1, and use the Three Steps to Feeling Good to redirect your negative thoughts into better-feeling thoughts.

Every time you disengage from the ego and lean toward your inner guide, you strengthen your ability to protect your vibration. You may still get sucked into negative thoughts from time to time, but the miracle is you will no longer believe in them. It will become easier and easier for you to stay in alignment with your inner guide so that it becomes your default to have fun and feel good.

WOULD YOU RATHER BE HAPPY OR BE RIGHT?

If you are someone who often finds yourself getting caught up in petty arguments or disagreements, make it a habit to pause and ask yourself this question, "Would I rather be happy or be right?" This simple question can completely change the way you approach arguments.

I used to be the person who insists on winning an argument. I was under the limiting belief that I will be happy after I "win" an argument. But despite "winning" the argument, I often find myself feeling drained after the high from "winning" fades away. But everything changed after I was introduced to this question. I now realize the only way to "win" an argument is to choose happiness over being right.

Remember, there is always a trade-off when it comes to energetic exchanges. When you hold on to the need to be right, you put your energetic vibration at risk. Besides lowering your own vibration, the words that come out of the heat of the argument can deeply wound other people. So, the next time you find yourself in an argument, use this question to remind yourself where your true priority lies.

YOU GOTTA BE SELFISH TO BE SELFLESS

When you start to apply these practices into your daily life, the people around you will take notice and may even accuse you of being selfish. Most people are afraid of change and this resistance applies to both positive and negative changes. Simply know that this is part of the course when you make a commitment to feel good. Instead of letting their nasty comments lower your energy, take them as signs of confirmation that your practices of protecting your vibration are working.

When someone takes proactive measures to protect their physical health, no one accuses them of being selfish. In fact, we celebrate people who honor their physical bodies and live healthy lifestyles. So why should it be any different when it comes to our energy? When you take actions to protect your energy, you are in no way depriving someone else of their energy.

Besides, if you are not selfish enough to intentionally protect your energy, you have nothing to give anyway. Your energy has the power to influence the energy around you due to the vibrational momentum caused by the Law of Attraction. By maintaining high vibration and positive energy, you can actually elevate those who are stuck in low vibration. So, get out there and own your newfound selfish title. Wear it like a badge of honor. The next time someone accuses you of being selfish with your energy, simply remind yourself that you can't pour from an empty cup.

CHAPTER 7: MIRACLES

When you commit to the practices in this book and embrace the habit of feeling good; signs, synchronicities, and miraculous shifts will begin to show up in your life. Your job is to look for them, acknowledge them as miracles, and accept your power as a miracle worker.

Many of us have put the word, *miracle*, on a pedestal and we are under the limiting belief that miracles can only happen to certain individuals. (Usually those who we think are better than us, godlier than us, or holier than us.) But this is due to our misunderstanding on what constitutes a miracle. I too, was under this limiting belief, until I came across the metaphysical text, *A Course In Miracles*. This book contains many nuggets of wisdom, and its teachings on miracles are extremely profound.

When most people think about miracles, they think of the miraculous events that were recorded in the Bible such as, when Jesus turned water into wine, or when Moses parted the Red Sea. These are indeed tremendous acts of miracles, but a miracle is not defined by its magnitude. *A Course In Miracles* tells us, "There is no order of difficulty among miracles. One is not "harder" or "bigger" than another. They are all the same." If you hold on to the limiting belief that miracles can only be performed by certain individuals, you give up your ability to experience miracles in your own life. And when you give up on miracles, you give up on manifestations. Because manifestations *are* acts of miracles.

The truth is there is no big or small when it comes to miracles.

From manifesting a career that you love, to releasing limiting beliefs that no longer serve you, every single step you take toward alignment with the Universe is a miracle. In fact, *A Course In Miracles* simply defines a miracle as a shift in perception. Every time you choose to let go of fear and come back to love; you experience a miracle.

If you want to live a life full of miracles, the solution is really simple. Simply open your eyes and look for them. Miracles are happening all around you; you just need to notice them. When you celebrate every sign, every synchronicity, and every manifestation as a miracle from the Universe and dismiss nothing as a coincidence, you will begin to live a miraculous life.

SIGNS FROM THE UNIVERSE

Miracles can show up in a lot of ways, but one of the most common ways is through a sign from the Universe. These signs can range from repeating numbers on your clock to a symbol of your favorite animal. Signs from the Universe often show up in subtle ways and they can easily be dismissed as coincidences. But when you accept these signs as guidance from the Universe, you open up another way to collaborate with the Universe.

Some spiritual students use signs as a way to ask for divine guidance on making decisions, but I believe the application of signs is even broader than that. Signs are the Universe's way of telling you to check if your energy is in alignment with love. Whenever you see a sign from the Universe, use it as a reminder to check your vibration by feeling into your current emotions. If you are feeling great and aligned with positive vibration, simply thank the Universe for this confirmation that you're on the right path. If you notice you are not feeling good or you are stuck in a place of misalignment, use this moment as your opportunity to reach for better-feeling thoughts.

My sign from the Universe is 1111 and it has guided me out of low vibration so many times. No matter what I am going through during the day, seeing my sign always brings me back to the present moment so I can realign and feel good again.

What happens if you don't know what your sign is? Don't worry, you can choose one right now. Don't overthink it and simply go with a number, symbol, or object that you resonate with. Once you have chosen your sign, declare it to the Universe using this prayer, "Universe, I choose (insert your sign) as my sign. I am ready to accept new forms of guidance." This powerful prayer is a sincere invitation for collaboration with the Universe. Now all you have to do is keep your eyes open and allow yourself to be guided.

APPRECIATE YOUR MIRACLES

The power of miracles doesn't necessarily lie in its magnitude but in how good it makes you feel. When you attribute a miracle to the God of your own understanding, you can feel good knowing that you are being guided and protected by a power greater than you. This spiritual connection catapults you into feelings of love, joy, and appreciation, all of which are emotions with the highest vibrations.

Miracles are not defined by the size of their physical outcomes. Your miracles can be as simple as finding a dollar bill on the ground or as major as finding your soulmate. What you need to do is to recognize each and every small win as a miracle so that you can get into the feelings of appreciation. The more you appreciate the miracles in your life, the more miracles you will manifest in your life. This is simply how the manifestation process works.

COINCIDENCES DO NOT SERVE YOU

You may still not be entirely sold on the concept of miracles. So, let's flip the coin and consider the alternative to miracles. If you choose to see a miracle as a mere coincidence, then that's all it is—a coincidence. An outcome that resulted from chance or luck that's beyond your control. Coincidences do not serve you; they do nothing for you emotionally and vibrationally.

But if you choose to see a coincidence as a miracle, you can strengthen your faith in the Universe, the same force that works with you to manifest your desires into reality. By believing in miracles, you can raise your vibration and feel good knowing you are being guided by a force of love that watches over you.

WE TEND TO FORGET MIRACLES

Many of us tend to focus our attention on the negative rather than the positive. We can be thriving in nine out of ten areas in our lives, yet we spend every waking moment obsessing over that one area that's lacking. A more scientific term for this phenomenon is the *negativity bias*. The *negativity bias* states that things of a negative nature have a greater effect on our psychological state than neutral or positive things, even when of equal intensity.

I can personally attest to this phenomenon. It takes conscious effort to not only *acknowledge* but to *appreciate* the miracles in your life. Otherwise, no matter how many miracles you experience, they will just end up being distant memories. Let me share with you my story of a life-changing miracle I experienced and how I was later guided to make it my spiritual proof.

It was April 23, 2018, an ordinary day at the office. My co-worker and I agreed to head out after lunch for a walk to check out this local food truck. After I finished my lunch around 1:00 p.m., my co-worker asked if I was ready to head out, but somehow my intuition compelled me to stay a bit longer to wrap up a conversation in the lunchroom.

When we finally decided to take a walk down the block to where the food truck was located. I saw an unusually large crowd of people gathered near the street intersection. When I walked closer and approached the commotion, I was mortified by the sight of several bodies lying on the sidewalk. It was a sight that I would never forget. Some people were unconscious, and others were being resuscitated by bystanders.

Later, I would come to find out that I walked directly into the aftermath of a mass murder, which is now known as the Toronto van attack. Just moments before I arrived, a man drove a van down a sidewalk and killed and injured dozens of pedestrians. The very same sidewalk where the food truck I was headed to was located. If I had been there five minutes earlier, I cannot imagine what would have happened. It was no coincidence that I felt compelled to stay a few minutes longer in the lunchroom. It was a miracle—a moment of divine protection from the Universe. At that moment, I was overwhelmed by feelings of love, gratitude, and appreciation.

Even though this miracle altered the trajectory of my life, it did not take long for me to revert to my old tendency of focusing on what's not working. The latest news on social media, the nine-to-five office grind, and the never-ending to-do lists just sucked me right back into the void of negativity.

It was not until two years later, when the legal proceedings of the case hit the news again, that I was reminded of this incredible moment of divine protection. I intuitively knew that this was guidance from the Universe. At that moment, I whole-heartedly acknowledged this event as a miracle from the Universe and I cemented this event as a miracle by writing it down in my journal. Now, whenever my small-mindedness gets the best of me, I can simply pick up my journal, appreciate my miracles, and feel better instantly, knowing that I'm being guided by a loving force that is greater than me.

Let my story be a warning of just how easy it is to lose sight of miracles when you stop looking for them. Ever since I wrote down that miracle in my journal, I have continued to add moments of synchronicity and spiritual guidance to my growing list of miracles. This list of miracles has accumulated over time to become my spiritual proof to confirm that I am indeed being guided by a higher power.

Now let me help you create your own journal for recording the miracles in your life. These steps will help you create the spiritual proof that you can use to lift you up when you are down and bring you back into the positive feelings of appreciation and love.

STEP 1: RECOGNIZE YOUR MIRACLES

Think back on your life and recall synchronicities, manifestations, or moments of protection—any situations where you felt the presence of a higher power.

Pick one moment that stands out to you and imagine how your life would be like if you knew that you were being guided all the time. Lean into how good it feels to be led by a force that's greater than you.

Affirm your ability as a miracle worker and welcome more miracles into your life by saying this prayer, "Thank you, Universe, for helping me recognize these moments as miracles. I am ready to experience a miraculous life."

Trust that by saying this prayer, you accept the Universe's invitation for collaboration, and you open the floodgates of miracles into your life.

STEP 2: CREATE A MIRACLE LOG

Create your Miracle Log by dedicating a journal to writing down your miracles. Your Miracle Log is a gratitude journal that is specifically dedicated to the higher power of your own understanding.

Because of our tendency to focus our attention on what's not working, it's very important to write down moments of miracles so that we don't forget about them.

Start by writing down the miracles that you recalled in Step 1. Afterward, you can add to the running list of miracles whenever you experience them in your life.

Remember the basic definition of a miracle is simply a shift in perception. No miracle is too small to be included in your Miracle Log. Make it a daily habit to write down all the moments where you felt supported, guided, or led by the Universe.

STEP 3: USE IT AS SPIRITUAL PROOF

Your Miracle Log will now serve as your spiritual proof to remind you that you are indeed being guided by a higher power.

Whenever you feel stuck in low vibration or you get impatient about something you're trying to manifest, simply pick up your Miracle Log and remind yourself how the Universe has supported you in the past.

Reviewing your past miracles is powerful because it allows you to assume the feelings of joy, love, and appreciation in the present moment. When you appreciate the miracles that happened in the past, you raise your energetic vibration in the present. Your Miracle Log helps you realign with the loving presence of the Universe so you can manifest even more miracles in the future.

A SHIFT IN PERCEPTION

Now that you have learned about miracles, I want to spend the next chapter talking about obstacles. Some people think that when you commit to a spiritual path, it means that you will never have to face any difficult situations or circumstances ever again. But that is not true, at least not entirely. Being spiritual *doesn't* guarantee that you will never have to face an obstacle again. But what it *does* guarantee is that you will never have to face an obstacle alone again.

When you have unwavering faith in the Universe, you can choose to see your obstacles from the lens of love. When you let love lead the way, you will be able to perceive obstacles as opportunities, difficulties as lessons, and enemies as assignments. Once you establish a spiritual connection with a God of your own understanding, you will no longer live in the darkness with fleeting moments of light. Instead, you will live in the light with fleeting moments of darkness. Turn the page and let the light in.

CHAPTER 8: OBSTACLES ARE OPPORTUNITIES

During my early 20s, I struggled with severe acne. It was one of the most challenging times in my life, but now I can see it as one of my most profound learning experiences. My acne severely affected my mental health and gave me social anxiety. Like most people, I had acne when I was a teenager, but I was convinced that my acne would go away as I get older. While this may be true for most people, this was not the case for me. It was tough to be the only one in the office to have acne and I couldn't help but compare myself to my peers. I held on to the belief that my skin "should" be clear now that I am past my teenage years. But this "should" mentality sent me into a negative spiral of controlling and obsessive behavior.

At first, I was determined to heal my skin on my own. I poured hundreds of dollars into buying expensive skin care products and I spent a lot of time researching ingredients and watching educational videos online. I also went to visit a dermatologist, but even the prescribed treatments didn't work because I kept interfering with my skin care routine. Like clockwork, every time I made some progress, I would end up back in the same place after a few weeks.

It got to a point where I was miserable, frustrated, and just done with trying to treat my skin on my own. This moment of defeat was another rock bottom moment for me. Because of what I previously went through with my diet, I quickly realized that this perceived obstacle was just a lesson for me to practice letting go of the outcome. This was my chance to let go of my "should" mentality and surrender to a higher power.

The moment I saw my acne as a lesson instead of an obstacle, everything changed. I booked another appointment with a dermatologist again but with a completely different mindset. I was willing to let go of my controlling tendencies and just let the prescribed medication do the work. Instead of self-sabotaging my skin care routine, I relaxed and trusted that the medication was enough to heal my skin. I let go of my limiting belief of how my skin "should" look like and I surrendered the outcome to the Universe.

During the course of the treatment, my skin went through ups and downs, but it was my faith in the Universe that got me through it. Instead of obsessing over how my skin "should" look like, I appreciated the progress I was making. By releasing my need to control the outcome, I was living out Step 5 of the Spiritual Manifestation Method which is to let go and allow. Spiritual surrender was the key to my manifestation.

In six months, my skin experienced drastic improvements. I went from having severe cystic acne to just the occasional pimple here and there. Even though the journey was tough from a physical standpoint, it taught me a great lesson on manifesting. I thank the Universe for teaching me the importance of getting out of my own way and the power of surrender. The moment I let go of my need to control, I gave myself the space I needed to heal.

YOUR PERSPECTIVE IS EVERYTHING

Just because you are on a spiritual path, it doesn't mean you will not encounter any obstacles in your life. Everyone goes through ups and downs in life, but the factor that determines whether you succumb to or overcome obstacles lies in how you choose to perceive them.

Two different individuals can go through the same experience but have two entirely different outcomes. Why? The answer lies in their *perceptions*. Imagine two people going on a roller coaster ride. The first individual enjoys thrill rides. The second individual is deathly afraid of heights. They can go through the same experience (the roller coaster ride) but have two completely different outcomes because of their perceptions. The first individual would feel exhilarated while the second individual would be in panic mode. This analogy can be applied to any other obstacle you face in life.

As a manifestor, you understand that you manifest what you think and feel. If you spend most of your time worrying about your obstacles, you will simply manifest more obstacles into your life. So, the only way out of obstacles is to redirect your attention to what you want and how you want to feel instead.

When you shift your perspective from fear to love, your external circumstances may not change right away. But the way you experience your external circumstances changes immediately. By proactively raising your vibrational frequency, you can step back and see the obstacle from a lens of love rather than a lens of fear. This is when you regain control of the manifestation process.

OBSTACLES ARE LESSONS FROM THE UNIVERSE

The Universe works in mysterious ways, and sometimes obstacles are divinely placed into your life so that you can learn an important spiritual lesson. When you perceive an obstacle with fear, you will just manifest more fear. But when you perceive an obstacle as a lesson, you can approach it from a place of faith. The Universe will never give you something more than you can handle.

A common misconception in the Law of Attraction community is that you attract your obstacles. This can be true in some circumstances, but it is a dangerous belief to subscribe to because it can send you into a downward spiral of blame and guilt. Instead of blaming yourself for how the obstacle came about, you are better off focusing on how you can move forward.

The key to manifesting is to always focus on what feels good. Use the tools that you have learned in this book to make sense of the perceived obstacle in front of you, reorganize your energy, and take the next best action so that you can make your way back into alignment with the Universe.

HEAL LIMITING BELIEFS

Obstacles are often the catalysts to healing our old limiting beliefs. Limiting beliefs can be difficult to unlearn because they can be deeply ingrained in the shadows of our subconscious minds. We tend to go about our lives and let these limiting beliefs run our lives in the background because we are too afraid to confront them. It is said that we are more afraid of our light than our darkness. But obstacles are often just what we need to shine a light on those limiting beliefs and bring them into our line of sight.

When you come face to face with your limiting beliefs, you have two choices. You can either cower in fear and let them run your life, or you can witness them with love and replace them with a new set of beliefs. The moment you realize that your limiting beliefs no longer serve you, you become free to replace them with new ones that do serve you. Go back to Chapter 2 and follow the 3-step method to release your limiting beliefs through self-forgiveness. Forgiveness is the antidote to pain and suffering.

THE OBSTACLE WILL SHOW UP AGAIN AND AGAIN

When you take a look back at the obstacles in your life, you will probably notice that there is a pattern. Whether it is a struggle to keep a steady job or a series of failed relationships, the same obstacle will keep showing up in your life until you are willing to learn the lesson behind it. Perhaps that job loss is your chance to pivot into a career that you enjoy instead. Maybe that sudden breakup is your opportunity to love yourself even more. There is a lesson in every obstacle as long as you are willing to learn it.

Just like in my struggle with acne, the problem kept coming back despite trying different treatments because I was not willing to let go of the outcome. But the moment I released my control and surrendered the outcome to the Universe, I was healed, both physically and mentally.

The obstacle will show up again and again until you are willing to confront it. The sooner you recognize an obstacle as a lesson in disguise. The sooner you can begin the healing process and make your way through it.

OBSTACLES STRENGTHEN YOUR MANIFESTATION PRACTICE

It is easy to manifest what you want when your life is going great and you have everything that you need. Your vibration is often a direct reflection of your external circumstances. So, when your life is going well, you naturally emit positive energy and attract positive outcomes. But what about when life is not going so well? Do you let your obstacles drag your energy down or do you rise above so you can manifest your way out of them?

If you can manifest miracles even amid challenging times, just think about what you can manifest when your life is thriving. When you see an obstacle as an opportunity to strengthen your manifestation practice, you can find comfort in knowing that your perceived challenges are just preparations for the manifestations that are yet to come.

So, don't run from your obstacles. Learn to embrace them with grace. Follow these three steps to accept your obstacles as opportunities.

STEP 1: ACCEPT YOUR ASSIGNMENT

The first step to overcoming an obstacle is to accept it as a spiritual assignment.

If you have been running away from an obstacle or brushing it under the carpet, this is your opportunity to shine a flashlight on it and come face to face with it.

The great thing about this step is it does not require you to do anything or make anything happen.

All it takes is a willingness to shift your perspective to see the obstacle as a lesson instead.

Say this prayer to accept your lesson, "Universe, thank you for helping me perceive this obstacle as a lesson. I welcome your guidance now."

STEP 2: SEE FROM THE LENS OF LOVE

Now that you have accepted your assignment, it is time to see it from the lens of love.

When you detour into the perspective of fear, you block your connection to your inner guide, so you end up taking action from a place of misalignment. Misaligned actions are backed by low vibration, so you will just end up manifesting even more negative outcomes.

But when you perceive your obstacle from the perspective of love, you realign yourself with the loving force of the Universe, and you allow yourself to be guided to the next best action. Aligned actions are backed by high vibration, so you will manifest more positive outcomes.

When you are feeling stuck in an obstacle and you are unsure of what to do next, ask yourself, "What would love do in this situation?" Remember that love is synonymous with God. We may have different interpretations of God, but love is universal. We have all experienced the energy of love in some way, shape, or form, so we know the immense power that it holds. The energy of love is the highest vibrational frequency you can embody, so trust that when you assume the perspective of love, you will manifest solutions of the highest good for all.

But you don't have to wait until you hit rock bottom to see from the lens of love. Practice letting love lead the way with the obstacles you encounter every day. Whether it's a petty argument with your significant other or a minor disagreement with a friend. Simply ask yourself, "What would love do right now?" and let love take over.

STEP 3: SURRENDER THE OUTCOME

The final step is to surrender the outcome to the Universe. After you have committed to taking action from the lens of love, all that is left to do is to have faith and trust that the Universe will deliver.

This echoes the Spiritual Manifestation Method that was introduced in Chapter 4. When you assume the energy of love, you are in the perfect position to receive your manifestation.

Although every obstacle is uniquely placed in your life to heal a specific limiting belief or old wound, the underlying lesson in all obstacles is to let go and allow. There are no limits when it comes to surrendering to a higher power. You can always surrender more.

A UNIVERSAL OBSTACLE

A universal obstacle that many of us face in this lifetime is related to finding our passion. We ask ourselves questions like, "What is my purpose in life? What is my *raison d'être*? How can I find a career that aligns with my passion?" This topic is especially relevant for my generation, where so many young people struggle to find meaning and fulfillment in their jobs. Besides sleeping, the second activity that we spend the most time on in our lives is our careers. So, I want to dedicate the next chapter to following your passion in life. Notice how I said *following* instead of *finding*. Because the truth is, you don't find your passion, your passion finds you.

CHAPTER 9: FOLLOW YOUR PASSION

For a long time, I regretted my decision of going to college for a business administration degree. After working a few jobs in the field, I knew deep down that I was not made to just be an accountant. No matter how hard I tried to convince myself to be grateful to even have a secure job, my intuition told me that there has got to be more to life than just numbers and spreadsheets.

When I embarked on my spiritual path, I intuitively felt the need to start sharing about my journey into the world of spirituality. I started a blog called *The Millennial Grind* and began to publish articles on manifestation and self-help. I have never considered myself a writer. In fact, a limiting belief that I often repeated to myself was, "I am not a creative person," hence my decision to study accounting at school. Despite having this limiting belief in the back of my mind, I went on to write and share what I have learned on my spiritual path.

My inner critic repeatedly tried to sabotage this idea by saying things like:

- Who are you to write a blog?
- You are not even good at writing.
- Do you even have time to run a blog?
- Your blog will never be successful.

- Why don't you put more effort into your real job instead?

But my intuition told me otherwise. Even though I wasn't getting that many views or making money from the blog, it felt so good to do something I was passionate about. The words came out of me effortlessly and it was therapeutic to affirm what I believed in by sharing it with the rest of the world. When I committed to the practice feeling good and reconnected with a higher power, my life changed radically for the better. I just knew that there were millions of people out there in the world who were stuck in the same position as I was who could greatly benefit from these messages.

After almost a year of blogging, my blog traffic started to pick up out of nowhere. My blog ended up reaching over one million readers during its second year of operations. Looking back at it now, I am not surprised this was the outcome that manifested. All along I was practicing the Spiritual Manifestation Method. I released all expectations and I simply let my good feeling emotions guide me throughout the blogging process. By focusing on how good these messages made me feel, I remained faithful that the Universe would bring these messages to those who need them when the time comes.

Let my story show you the power of listening to your intuition, which is always guiding you toward your passion. The voice of your inner critic may be loud, but the voice of your intuition is even louder *if* you choose to listen to it. When you do something and it feels good, natural, or right to you, that is your cue that you are on the right track toward your passion. You don't have to figure it all out right here or right now. When you make feeling good your highest priority, you can just sit back and let the Universe catch up with your dreams.

YOUR INTUITION IS GUIDING YOU

The key to following your passion is to let your intuition guide you toward what feels good. Just like how everyone has their own likes and dislikes, everyone has their own passion and purpose in life. And the only way to know that purpose is to listen to that still small voice within you.

Many people have the misunderstanding that your passion must be something that you are good at. But you can't get better at something until you know what that "something" is. The longer you resist your intuition, the longer you wait until you discover your passion.

Take a moment now to look at the areas in your life where you have the most fun in. Maybe you like to dance. Maybe you love doing makeup. Or perhaps you enjoy cooking for your loved ones. Put an asterisk beside any hobby or skill that you genuinely enjoy. You don't even need to be good at it. You just need to have fun and feel good. When you are feeling good, you are in alignment with the Universe. And when you are in alignment with the Universe, you can manifest everything you want and more.

STOP PUSHING AND START FEELING

A common mistake people make when trying to discover their passion is to hop from one thing to the next without consulting their inner guide. This is the perfect recipe for burnout because you are looking for passion in all the wrong places.

When you think that your passion is something that exists *outside* of you, you will feel the need to push and shove in order to find it. This creates resistance against the voice of your intuition who is always guiding you toward your passion through how you feel.

The only way to find your passion is to stop pushing and start feeling. You don't need to search for your passion because it is already *within* you. All you need to do is listen to your inner wisdom and lean into the things that bring you joy.

WE LIVE IN A UNIVERSE OF ABUNDANCE

Many of us struggle with the limiting belief that we live in a universe where opportunities are limited and resources are finite. This is a common excuse that we use to procrastinate on pursuing our dreams and passions. We say things like, "This has already been done before," or "Who am I to do this?" which suffocates our passions with negativity before we have the opportunity to manifest something great.

But the truth is we live in a universe of abundance. It's true that many things have been done before. But it is also true that many things have not been done by *you*. Every one of us has a special gift that we can offer the world. The only way to discover this gift is to follow the gentle guidance of our intuition. Your intuition is always guiding you and leading you toward what feels good. It's time to listen. It's time to stop playing small and manifest what you have always wanted to do in life.

YOU DON'T NEED TO FIGURE IT ALL OUT

The great thing about following your passion is you don't need to figure it all out right now. Your passion is not a for-profit business. You don't need to worry about how you can make money from it. You don't need to worry about how to promote your products and services. You don't even need to worry about the number of likes you get on social media. Your only job right now is to have fun and feel good.

Recognize that the need to plan ten steps ahead is just the voice of your ego trying to sabotage your good feelings. Remember that we are all energetic beings, so it is very easy for others to sense inauthentic energy from a mile away. Trust that when you focus on feeling good, you are primed to manifest everything you need and more. Let your passion elevate your spirit so much that other people can't help but be attracted to your light. When you let go of the need to control the outcome and allow inspiration to take the lead, abundance is sure to follow.

TURN COMPARISON INTO INSPIRATION

With the advent of social media and the rise of people flaunting what they have on the internet, it's easy to fall into the trap of comparison and feel inadequate. When you are jealous of what someone else has, you are reinforcing the fact that you do *not* have what they have. Jealousy is an emotion with low vibration, so it creates resistance against what you want. And by the Law of Attraction, you will continue to *not* have it as long as you are stuck in jealousy.

But I want you to recognize that the act of comparison in itself is not bad. After all, comparison is the catalyst that leads to growth and innovation. The key to using comparison for good is to turn it into inspiration instead. Whenever you see someone who has something that you want, try celebrating their success as if it was your own. Imagine how good it feels to have what they have and tune into this feeling during your visualization practice. You can also choose to see it as a confirmation from the Universe that it is possible to manifest your dreams and goals, whatever they may be.

COMPLAINING GETS YOU NOWHERE

The best way to follow your passion is to stop complaining about where you currently are and start focusing on where you want to be instead.

When you spend your time complaining about your current situation, you are focusing on all the negative things you are experiencing and attracting more negative outcomes into your reality. When you complain about how you are stuck in a career you hate, you are telling the Universe that you want to be stuck where you are.

If you are feeling unfulfilled by your career, that is actually a great indicator that you have not completely blocked off the guidance from your intuition. The reason why you feel this disturbance in your heart is because you know deep down you are supposed to be doing something else instead. When you know what you *don't* want to do in life, you are presented with the perfect opportunity to clarify what it is that you *do* want to do. Instead of resenting where you are currently at in life, be grateful that it is pointing you toward where you are supposed to be instead.

THERE ARE NO WRONG PATHS

Another roadblock toward following your passion is letting your past decisions define who you are. A lot of people give up on their passion because they studied the "wrong" program at school, or they have already invested too much time into the "wrong" career path. When your thoughts are consumed by regrets about the past, you assume that negative energy in the present and you block the opportunities that are in the future.

The only way to snap out of the grasp of regrets is to recognize that there are no wrong decisions in life. The belief that there are "right" or "wrong" decisions is simply the ego's way of making you stuck in the past. Embrace the fact that you are exactly where you are supposed to be. Honor your path for giving you direction on where you should go next.

THE WORLD NEEDS YOUR PASSION

Following your passion is not just about serving you. It's about serving the world. This is why it is so important for you to listen to your intuition and allow yourself to be guided toward what you are meant to do. If you think that your particular passion doesn't serve the world, I will need you to think again. Following your passion is not about what you do, it's about who you become. When you live a life that is aligned with your truth, you bring high vibrational energy into every single aspect of your life. In this positive energetic state, you are able to manifest outcomes that elevate your spirit and the spirits of those around you.

When you follow your passion, you radiate an energy of joy and positivity that can be felt by everyone around you. This is the reason why people who have realized their passions often also become influential leaders in the world with a large following. The energy of passion is so magnetic that it has the ability to inspire those around you to follow their passions as well.

Every time you ignore that gentle tug from your intuition, you are not only doing a great disservice to *yourself* but also to *those around you*. Now is the time to stop chasing and start listening. The world is waiting for you to follow your passion.

CHAPTER 10: BE THE LIGHT

I was only in the early stages of writing this manuscript, but I already knew I had to end the book with a chapter on how to be the light in the midst of darkness. We live in a world where the attention is focused on everything that is going wrong rather than everything that is going right. Simply take a moment to go on social media or turn on the news and you will be immediately assaulted by negative events and injustices that are occurring all over the planet.

As you have learned throughout this book, the key to manifesting lies in how you feel. This is why feeling good is so important if you want to manifest a life beyond your wildest dreams. If you follow the concepts in this book, you will experience a radical transformation in your life and you will become a beacon of light to those around you. When you commit to the practice of feeling good, you become a flashlight in a sea of darkness.

When you devote yourself to the practice of manifestation, you inevitably sign up to become a lightworker. A lightworker's job is not to preach or convince other people to follow their spiritual practices. A lightworker's only job is to simply *be* the light. Let your light shine so brightly that those who are lost in the darkness can't help but come to you to learn how they too can bear this light.

LET YOUR ENERGY SPEAK FOR ITSELF

When you first discover the joy of manifesting, it is natural to want to share it with all of your friends and family. But you need to keep in mind that not everyone is ready to receive this message. As you have learned in Chapter 6, protecting your energy is one of the most important things you can do as a manifestor. If you are not careful with how you bring this message to your loved ones, you put yourself at risk of lowering your vibrational stance and weakening your faith in the Universe.

When I surrendered to a higher power and committed to feeling good, my life did a one-eighty and shifted for the better. I began manifesting miracles all around me and synchronicities showed up in all areas of my life. I was eager to share this message with everyone I loved including my mom. But my attempts to share my spiritual experiences fell on deaf ears. She had high resistance due to her religious beliefs, so she completely shut out my messages. Every time I brought up this topic, it always resulted in disagreements and arguments. Although I initiated these conversations with good intentions, I walked away feeling drained every time. But I'm thankful for these experiences because these negative feelings were just the guidance I needed from my inner guide. I knew that I needed to change my approach if I wanted to protect my vibration and alignment with the Universe.

I decided to let my actions speak for themselves. I realized that my job as a lightworker is not to *teach* but to *demonstrate*. Energy speaks louder than words. My only responsibility is to focus on my vibration so that I can manifest miracles that elevate myself and those around me. Just as how my inner guide has the power to guide me back to my truth, I need to have faith in the inner guides that are at work in the people around me. Your spiritual practice is like the sun. The sun does not need to announce its light to the world; it simply shines and everything in the solar system benefits from it.

SPIRITUALITY IS AN INSIDE JOB

Another thing to keep in mind is that spirituality is an inside job. You can't fight other people's battles for them. Everyone is on their own spiritual path and no external forces can change them if they are not ready to be changed. After all, the first step to change is to want it.

It can be frustrating to watch the people in your life get stuck in vicious cycles, but those recurring obstacles may just be what they need to surrender to a higher power. The most loving thing you can do in these situations is to raise your vibration even higher. By strengthening your own connection to the Universe, you become a shining example of how good life can be when you are in alignment with a higher power.

TRUST THE TIMING OF THE UNIVERSE

There is this saying in the Buddhist tradition that says, "When the student is ready, the teacher will appear." As you commit to your manifestation practice, you will become a teacher to those around you. Currently, they may not see you as a teacher figure, but that is only because they are not ready to become students yet. The Universe works in mysterious ways, so all you have to do is trust in the timing of the Universe. Just like how you were guided to read this book on manifesting, trust that those who are ready to learn will be guided to their teachers when the time comes.

But that doesn't mean you can't do anything right now to prepare for that opportunity of teaching. Here are three pieces of advice when it comes to teaching others about your spiritual practice.

STEP 1: TO TEACH IS TO DEMONSTRATE

A Course in Miracles says, "To teach is to demonstrate." Teaching is not about lecturing and forcing your beliefs on others. The true meaning of teaching is to lead by example. When you make a commitment to feel good and co-create your reality with the Universe, you also sign up to become a teacher.

The best way to teach others about manifestation is to demonstrate it in your own life. Your actions and positive shifts in energy will be ten times more effective than your words, especially to those who have resistance to spiritual beliefs.

Simply live out your truth of feeling good and have faith that those who are ready to learn will come to you in their own time.

STEP 2: LET THEM COME TO YOU

When you make feeling good your highest priority, your life will change radically. You will experience more joy, happiness, and abundance than ever before. Miracles and synchronicities will happen all around you. Your positive energy will make your light shine so brightly that the people in your life can't help but notice these positive changes in your life.

As you manifest more and more miracles in your life, the people around you will want to approach you so they can learn from you. When you devote your energy to strengthening your own spiritual practice, even those who are initially resistant to your beliefs will lower their resistance and accept your newfound faith in the Universe.

STEP 3: IGNITE THE SPARK

When someone is ready and willing to hear your message, that is your opportunity to point them in the right direction. The spark of God is within all of us in the form of the inner guide, and you can be the one to help others ignite it. The best way to do this is to share your own experiences. Personal experiences are very relatable so they will resonate deeply with whoever you share them with.

- **Share Your Story:** Tell them about your spiritual journey and how your life has changed when you committed to feeling good. Your story doesn't have to be life-changing in order to make an impact. All experiences are inherently valuable. What matters is the authenticity and passion you bring to your listeners. Let your vibes speak louder than your words.

- **Share Your Practices:** Share the spiritual practices that you find helpful for aligning with your higher power. Tell them about your favorite methods for raising your vibration or the rituals you do to protect your energy. You don't need to get into the nitty-gritty details. Simply focus on how fun these practices are and how good they make you feel.
- **Share Your Resources:** Talk about your favorite books, podcasts, and teachers on spirituality. Open them up to the wonderful world of manifestation and the resources that are available to new seekers.

Remember that your job as a lightworker is not to force spiritual teachings on people. By sharing your personal experiences, you gently help others remember their own connection to their inner guide. This inner guide exists within every single individual. No matter what kind of obstacles they have been through. No matter how many limiting beliefs they are carrying. No matter what kind of situation they are currently facing. This spiritual connection may be weakened but it can never be broken. Trust that by leading them on a spiritual path, the Universe will guide them to where they need to go next.

MAKE FEELING GOOD YOUR HIGHEST PRIORITY

The moment you decide to embark on a spiritual path, it becomes a lifelong journey. The road ahead will be long and sometimes winding, but you will soon realize that there are no right or wrong paths to take as long as you commit to make feeling good your highest priority. Every new belief that you *learn* and every limiting belief that you *unlearn* brings you closer and closer to the truth of who you are—which is love.

When you commit to the practices in this book, it doesn't mean you will not face any obstacles, challenges, or difficulties in your life. Sometimes, the Universe will place a detour into your life so that you can heal an old wound or discard a limiting belief. But when you truly commit to the practice of feeling good, you will be able to shift your mindset and perceive the situation in a more loving way. You can step back and recognize that this obstacle in front of you is actually a spiritual lesson from the Universe. When you remember that feeling good is your birthright, you realign with the higher power that exists within you, and creative solutions will be revealed to you. You can take action from a place of confidence, ease, and faith, knowing that you are always in co-creation with the Universe.

Writing this book has been a cathartic experience for me and I hope these messages resonate with you. I want you to know that just by finishing this book, you have already created a radical shift in your life, and you are more than ready to claim your power as a co-creator with the Universe. It is my wish that you make the methods in the book a daily practice that you will come back to over and over again. But if you were to only take away one thing after reading this entire book, it would be the mantra—it's good to feel good.

ACKNOWLEDGMENTS

I thank my readers for their continued support and for allowing me to do what I love.
I thank my parents for all they've given me and for always being there for me.
I thank the Universe for the loving guidance and for being my source of inspiration.

ABOUT THE AUTHOR

Kenneth Wong (@manifestwithken) is the founder of The Millennial Grind, a self-help and spirituality blog founded in 2019. What started as just a space to share what he has learned in his journey into manifestation, quickly grew into an online community that serves readers from all over the world. In 2020, his articles have been read more than one million times. In 2021, Kenneth released his first book, Feeling Good. For more on his work, visit millennial-grind.com.

NOTES

Printed in Great Britain
by Amazon

64856006R00061